BICYCLE PEOPLE

BICYCLE PEOPLE

BY
ROLAND C. GEIST

FOREWORD BY
DR. PAUL DUDLEY WHITE

A
Published by **ACROPOLIS BOOKS Ltd.** ● Washington D.C. 20009

Acropolis Books are distributed in

Canada
by Carlton House, Ontario, Canada

Europe and the British Commonwealth
by Paul Maitland, Ltd., Kent, England

Japan
by Atlantic Book Service, Tokyo

Pakistan
by SASI Ltd., Karachi

Elsewhere in Asia and Australia
by ICTO PTE Ltd., Singapore

Library of Congress Cataloging in Publication Data

```
Geist, Roland C
   Bicycle people.

   Bibliography:  p.
   Includes index.
   1.  Bicycles and tricycles--History.  2.  Bicycles and
tricycles--Miscellanea.  I.  Title.
GV1040.5.G44     796.6'09     78-13567
ISBN 0-87491-272-3
```

ACKNOWLEDGMENTS

The author wishes to express thanks to the many friends who have helped in the preparation of this book. Special thanks are extended to the following:

G. Donald Adams
Sandra Alpert
Annette Friedman
Elizabeth Geist
Phyllis W. Harmon
James J. Hayes
William Jenack
Dr. Paul B. Mac Cready
William Oakley
Lorne Shields
Dinah Southern
G. Herbert Stancer
Dick Swan
Jack Wiley

Best wishes
from
Paul E. White
July, 1957

DEDICATION

To the late Dr. Paul Dudley White, the eminent cardiologist of Boston, our modern pioneer in the safe bicycle path campaign and whose prescription for America's health was, "Ride a Bicycle."

CONTENTS

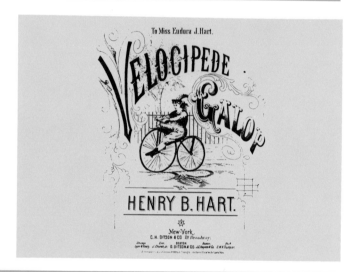

10

FOREWORD

Roland Geist has been one of the great names of the bicycling world of our day and is still an active practitioner of the art. He has been an inspiration to many thousands of us, both young and old, and it is a pleasure to honor him with this foreword.

Paul Dudley White
Boston, January 29, 1972

PUCK'S SUGGESTION TO HIS REVEREND FRIENDS.

If the Wheelmen Won't Go to Church, the Churches Will Have to Come to the Wheelmen.

INTRODUCTION

"... It won't be a stylish marriage
I can't afford a carriage,
But you'll look sweet
Upon the seat
Of a bicycle built for two!"
        Popular song, circa 1890

"America's Favorite Bicycle" --
Schwinn

"La Bicyclette de France
Championne du Monde" --
Gitane

"Since 1887 ... America's
FIRST Bicycle.
-- Columbia

Bicycle Advertising Slogans,
1978

BICYCLE PEOPLE is -- to risk being sentimental -- a work of love on my part. I have been fascinated by bicycles for most of my life.

In this book, I profile leaders in the world of bicycles; the inventors and developers who pioneered them; the tourists who made bicycling an adventurous means of travel; the daring racers who captured national and international enthusiasm for bicycling as a sport; the famous wheelwomen; the show folk, circus performers and stunt drivers who made bicycling a a festive spectacle. *BICYCLE PEOPLE* also chronicles lesser known people who celebrated bicycling through their art, stories and poetry, songs, plays and films.

The illustrations were selected from many thousands I have collected for more than a half century. Among historical accounts of those people, places and events which contributed to bicycle history I have intermingled personal reminiscences. My hope is that you -- reader and rider (hopefully, both!) -- may share in my enjoyment of the world of bicycles. I am grateful to the many friends who have helped in obtaining information and pictures.

If you have been entertained by this book and are stimulated to further reading, I will be happy indeed with my years of research.

        Roland C. Geist

ALBERT AUGUSTUS POPE, THE FIRST AMERICAN BICYCLE MANUFACTURER
Colonel Pope, as he was known to the cycling world, was elected to the American Bicycle Hall of Fame just a hundred years after the founding of his company.
Courtesy Columbia Manufacturing Company

CERTIFICATE OF WARRANTY SIGNED BY POPE

1
THE
INVENTORS

NO ONE PERSON INVENTED THE BICYCLE. ITS most common predecessor, the world over, is the hobby horse. The bicycle shares, of course, an origin with all man's dreams for a mechanical contrivance for self-propulsion. "See how the wings, striking against the air, bear up the heavy eagle in the thin air on high," wrote Leonardo da Vinci in 1486 in his researches into the mechanical possibility of human flight. From such genius, and more to follow, were eventually realized the automobile, the airplane, the spaceship -- and the bicycle.

The scientific minds of the English, French, German and Americans were paramount in improving the hobby horse into the efficient, versatile and popular machine of today. It would require literally volumes to name all the inventors and inventions contributing to development of the modern bicycle. (My own research library contains seven volumes of English patent specifications and five volumes of the American digest of cycle patents!) But let us examine briefly the outstanding inventors, the improvements they contributed, and the leading bicycle manufacturers of the past century:

• *De Sivrac,* a Frenchman, invented the "Celerifers" in 1790. It featured a primitive wooden bar with a padded saddle and wheels. (Unfortunately, riders were at a disadvantage because it couldn't be steered easily.)

• *Baron von Drais* of Sauerbrun, Germany, invented an improved hobby horse that could be steered by the front wheel. He used the contraption in traveling about forest lands he supervised. In 1818, he obtained a patent for the device, which he called the "Draisienne." It enjoyed a measure of popularity in France, England and America.

• *Kirkpatrick MacMillan,* a Scottish blacksmith, was the first to fit pedals to the bicycle. In 1839, he attached cranks to the rear axle of the machine. Most historians credit MacMillan with inventing the bicycle -- and some accord him the dubious credit, as well, of being the first rider to hit a pedestrian.

• *Pierre Michaux* of Paris and his workman, *Pierre Lallement,* fitted pedals to the front wheel of the hobby horse. It is disputed as to which man deserves credit for this first forward step in the chain of inventions. Lallement left the employ of Michaux, went to New Haven in America and obtained a United States patent in 1886 for the new model. Michaux died in Paris in 1883. In 1894, the French people elected a monument to his memory at Bar-le-Duc, near Verdun; the French consider him "the father of the bicycle."

• *James Starley* of England invented the famous "Ariel" bicycle -- better known as the "Ordinary" or "Penny Farthing." For a decade it was popular in many countries, despite some impracticalities: it was difficult to mount and dismount, and had a tendency, when hitting an obstruction, of causing the rider to take a dangerous front fall -- what we bicyclists achingly call "a header." (Back in 1916, I rode one of these high-wheelers in a bicycle race at a Crotona Park, New York, Bicycle Festival. I lost the mile event and I also took a header.)

In 1885, Starley produced a prototype of the modern safety bicycle which he called "The Rover." At the time, he and other inventors were busy producing tandems, tricycles, and quadricycles which achieved some popularity.

Starley is considered the greatest bicycle inventor of England -- "father of the British cycle industry" -- and in 1884 was honored with a monument in his native Coventry. English bicycle historian Horace Wilton Bart-

leet established in Coventry a public museum of historic cycles; the museum contains examples of all the bicycles made by Coventry manufacturers. I visited this great collection a few years ago, and I recommend it to all bike lovers.

Albert Augustus Pope

Colonel Albert Augustus Pope, America's first and greatest bicycle manufacturer, was born in Boston, May 26, 1843. He served in the Civil War and was honorably discharged as a lieutenant colonel.

At the Philadelphia Centennial Exposition in 1886, Colonel Pope became fascinated with some English high-wheel bicycles and decided on the spot that this was the product that he would manufacture and sell. He made his first bicycle in Boston in 1887 and named it the "Columbia." In 1878, he moved his factory to Hartford. Colonel Pope's enterprise prospered from the start — in a few years his bicycle empire spread to 4,000 sales agencies around the country, with offices in London, Paris and Hamburg. In 1900, he again moved his factory, still within Connecticut, but this time to Westfield, where it remains today.

Colonel Pope was a major force in the sport of bicycling in America. He established the Boston Bicycle Club and the League of American Wheelmen. He fostered the famous "Wheel Around the Hub," a delightful bicycle tour around the City of Boston, an event enjoyed by thousands of bicyclists to the present day. In fact, up until a few years ago some of the early riders of the tour, now in their 80's and 90's, rode around the course in cars, the veterans sharing their memories with the nostalgia buffs of the new era.

Aside from his contribution to advanced technology in mettallurgy, Colonel Pope was a pioneer in the good roads movement. Considered the father of this movement, Pope underwrote the expenses for a course in road construction established at the Massachusetts Institute of Technology.

A man of many enduring good works, Colonel Pope died in 1909.

Other Pioneers of
the American Bicycle Industry

• *Albert H. Overman.* President and founder of the Overman Wheel Company, he visited and studied bicycle manufacture in England and France. He also designed and produced the popular "Victor" cycles.

• *Harold Dwight Corey.* Born in Brookline, Massachusetts, on January 25, 1864, he established an agency which imported and sold the English Rudge Bicycles. He was also a founding member of the early Boston Bicycle Club.

16

THE EVOLUTION OF THE BICYCLE, FROM 1819 TO 1928
By Carl W. Mitman

Courtesy of the United States National Museum

1. "Draisienne" or Hobby Horse	1819	6. "American Star"	1885
2. Lellement "Velocipede"	1869	7. Starley "Rover"	1885
3. J. K. Starley "Ariel"	1873	8. Lady's "Victoria"	1887
4. Columbia "Ordinary"	1885	9. Snyder "De Luxe"	1928
5. Humber "Racing Ordinary"	1885		

**THE GOSSAMER CONDOR ON ITS
KREMER PRIZE FLIGHT,
AUGUST 23, 1977**
The pilot was Bryan Allan.
Courtesy of Dr. Paul B. MacCready, the inventor

• *Albert G. Spalding.* He founded the great American Sporting Goods Company which specialized in baseball equipment and later in bicycle manufacture. A. G. Spalding and Brothers had offices in New York and Chicago; they were also the American sales agents for the English Humber bicycles.

• *H. B. Smith.* A United States Senator and Member of Congress from New Jersey, he showed great interest in machinery and established a $300,000 bicycle plant in Smithville (near Atlantic City). He conceived and manufactured the Star bicycle, a high-wheel with a small wheel in front, introducing it in May, 1881. (While safer to ride than the high-wheel ordinary, the model was not very popular.)

• *Herbert W. Gaskel.* This bicycle pioneer was born in Liverpool and worked with the Coventry Machine Company in England. He was the United States manager of the company.

• *Thomas B. Jeffery.* From Chicago, he toured England studying that country's bicycle manufacturing methods. He returned to the United States and specialized in making rims and tires. Later, with a partner, R. Philip

18

Gormully, the two invented many improvements in bicycle parts. The Gormully and Jeffery factory produced the popular Rambler bicycle equipped with G. and J. pneumatic tires. They advertised their pneumatic-tired bicycles as "The Acme of Comfort."

• *J. B. Dunlop.* This Englishman patented the pneumatic bicycle tire in 1888. It had been patented in 1845 by R. W. Thompson, but Thompson did not commericalize his new product. The air tire provided comfort and speed for the cyclist and was a tremendous step forward in bicycling. The old high-wheels had solid rubber tires. Among other accessories invented to improve cycling were ball bearings, easy riding chains, coaster brakes, gear shifts, improved saddles, lamps and cyclometers.

• *Alexander Moulton.* In the 1960's, this English engineer presented to the world the first newly designed bicycle in more than 70 years. After four years of experimentation, he produced a design with an improved suspension system and small wheels which brought greater maneuverability and comfort. The bicycle could also be adjusted for men, women and children. The "Stowaway" model, equipped with a coaster brake, may easily be taken apart and carried in a car, train or boat.

In 1978, Great Britain issued a commemorative set of postage stamps honoring the centenary of the famous Cyclists' Touring Club and the British Cycling Federation. The stamps portrayed four outstanding bicycles in the history of cycling.

The Modern Bicycles of the 1970's

The most popular bicycle of this decade is the ten-speed racer. It requires very little energy for hill climbing and offers pleasurable downhill coasting.

• Young people seem to prefer the high-rise or motocross small-wheel models.

• For commuting, service cycling and load carrying, the up-bar coaster brake models are efficient.

• Folding bicycles are practical for tourists who wish to use autos, trains, buses, boats, or planes en route to cycling areas.

• Track racers usually ride custom-made lightweight machines with high fixed gears and a short wheelbase.

• Unicycles are preferred by circus and show business people.

Dr. Paul Mac Cready
Our Greatest Modern Inventor
of Self-Powered Flight

Can man, under his own power, achieve flight? Leonardo thought it was possible. In this century, Dr. Paul MacCready has made that possibility a reality.

On August 23, 1977, Dr. MacCready saw his new invention, the "Gossamer Condor," make aviation history. The Gossamer Condor, a human-powered airplane, was piloted successfully by champion bicycle racer Bryan Allen at Shaffer Airport in California to win the $86,000 Kremer Prize offered by the Royal Aeronautical Society. The attempt at human-powered flight had been made unsuccessfully many times over the last 50 years by scientists of Austria, England, France, Germany and Japan.

Dr. MacCready, president of Aero Vironment Inc., and now a resident of Pasadena, was born in New Haven, Connecticut. As a youth he became interested in soaring. In 1947, he received his B.S. degree in physics from Yale. In 1948, he won his M.S. in physics and, in 1952, a Ph.D. in aeronautics from the California Institute of Technology. In 1956, he won the International Soaring Championships, and he has pioneered the use of aircraft to study weather phenomena.

What is the Gossamer Condor? Well, it is much like its name. A craft of diaphanous and fragile beauty, it weighs 70 pounds, has a 96-foot wing span and is 30 feet in length. It cost $30,000 in labor and materials to build. In the record-setting flight, the Gossamer Condor took 22.5 seconds to complete the official circuit—a figure eight course around pylons a half-mile apart, with a ten-foot high hurdle at the begining and end. The speed was between 10 and 11 miles an hour. Pilot Allen generated one-third of a horsepower to fly the plane.

Dr. MacCready's work at man-powered flight continues with more challenges. He reportedly has offered a cash prize for the first man-powered flight across the English Channel.

For his efforts so far, Dr. MacCready was elected unanimously to the American Bicycle Hall of Fame in New York. The first Gossamer Condor has been donated to the Smithsonian Institution in Washington, D.C.

Thomas Stevens

THOMAS STEVENS, THE SPECIAL CORRESPONDENT OF *OUTING*
He was the first to cycle around the world on a high wheel bicycle.
Courtesy of *Outing*

2
THE TOURISTS

IN THE PAST HUNDRED YEARS OF BICYCLING, two events have captured world interest. They were the daring around-the-world high bicycle tour of Thomas Stevens and the phenomenal speed record of "Mile-A-Minute Murphy".

Thomas Stevens started from San Francisco on April 22, 1884 on his high Columbia cycle and after many hardships and privations arrived in Boston, August 5, 1884. Here he met and contracted with Colonel Pope to write of his experiences for *Outing* magazine. On April, 1885 he left by steamer for Liverpool, England. His route was via London, Paris, Munich, Vienna, Belgrade, Constantinople, Teheran, Delhi, Agra, Benares, Shanghi,

PRESIDENT CARTER AND HIS BICYCLE
Photo by Kightlinger, The White House

Kobe, and Yokahama, then via ship to San Francisco, ending his grand adventure on December 17th, 1886.

On his triumphal return, Tom Stevens was tendered a banquet by the Bay City Wheelmen at the Baldwin Hotel, San Francisco on January 11, 1887. A poem was composed in his honor by Sam Booth as follows:

"You have heard of the famous steeds of old
    And the famous men who rode them -
The steeds of which old Homer told
    And the heroes who bestrode them;
Of Castor and Pollax's mystic steeds
    In MacCauley's classic story
And how they helped the Romans win
    Undying fame and glory.
Hurrah for brave Tom Stevens then
    Be every wheelman shouting,
Who takes a spin around the earth
    Just for a little Outing,
And here's to Tommy's faithful steed
    Who, wheres's ever he'd roam,
Yet never failed him in his need
    And brought him safely home.

And when their statues are raised on high,
    And every wheelman's throat is dry,
With beaker in hand be this their cry,
    Wherever the cycler's flag unfurled
"Here's to the king of the cycling world,
    And here's to the steed that bore him forth
And carried him safely 'round the earth."

Tom Stevens detailed his adventure in a two volume book *Around the World on a Bicycle* which was published by Charles Scribner's Sons. Another daring cyclist by the name of Lenz attempted to follow the Stevens tour, but he disappeared soon after he toured Turkey. During the past years at least six others have made the ride and have written up their thrilling stories. According to the Unicycling Society of America, one member is now in training to attempt this tour on one wheel.

Thomas Stevens has been elected to the American Bicycle Hall of Fame where his name and picture are enshrined for posterity. Dr. Irving A. Leonard, historian of the Wheelmen, has published an interesting short account of the Stevens story. During the summer of 1965, I had the pleasure of following the Stevens route around

22

OUR CYCLING ARTIST, NORMAN ROCKWELL
He is shown here with Mrs. Rockwell cycling in the Berkshires.
Courtesy of Norman Rockwell

the world via airplane in 50 days. Is it possible that the future will see a man tour the world in a Gossamer Condor, bicycle airplane?

After his world tour, Thomas Stevens competed in a 24 hour bicycle race against C.J. Young, a professional racer. This race cost him his amateur standing and membership in the League of American Wheelmen.

Touring Today

Sports Surveys and Bicycling

According to a recent survey by *U. S. News and World Report* listing the 25 sports involving the most participants in 1977, bicycling, with 76,000,000 active devotees, ranked second only to swimming.

Another survey by *Bicycling* showed the popularity of the various types of cycling:

touring	55.29%
recreational riding	23.50%
commuting	14.9 %
racing	6.4 %

Cyclists wanting to join a club may wish to know how many fellow members they will find in the various clubs. The approximate number of members are:

American Youth Hostels	70,000
Cyclists Touring Club	28,000
League of American Wheelmen	10,000
International Bicycle Touring Society	600

(Note: The American Youth Hostel totals include hiking, camping, sailing, skiing, skating and boating as well as just biking.)

These statistics show the popularity of associations for bike riders today and the great number of people who identify themselves proudly as "bicycle people."

Touring Clubs

The Story of Our First Bicycle Club

Compiled from an article appearing in *The Wheelman* of March 1883 written by a founder member and early president Charles E. Pratt.

On February 11, 1878, fourteen high-wheel cyclists met to organize the famous Boston Bicycle Club. Among its

23

early members were merchants, business executives, salesmen, students at Harvard, lawyers, clerks, architects and a physician.

The first clubrooms were located at 178 Devonshire Street, on the fifth and sixth floors. (It was observed that those members who used the elevators least were excellent hill climbers.) In November 1879, the club moved to commodious headquarters at 40 Providence Street with elegant clubrooms, a reading room, a library and a wheel room with lockers. The members also selected a club costume consisting of seal brown corduroy jacket and breeches with a helmet type of cap. The Wheelmen of today, an organized group of modern high riders, wear similar attire.

The first club run occurred on March 9, 1878, from Boston to Brookline. 1882 was especially memorable because seven members rode 102 ½ miles in 12 hours and 6 minutes. In 1878 the "amateur" question agitated the club; it was finally agreed that any rider who was in the sport for money or competed with professionals lost his amateur status.

A Wheel Around the Hub;
America's First Organized Bicycle Tour

This unique tour, sponsored by the Boston Bicycle Club, was organized on February 11, 1878.

About 27 riders in their blue uniforms started this grand tour on September 11, 1879. Charles E. Pratt was the tour captain, and was later elected to the League of American Wheelmen presidency. The run started in Boston when the Captain Pratt sounded "Boots and Saddles" on his bugle. The route led through sections teeming with historical associations. The first day's run was through Jamaica Pond, Dedham, and Readville (including a climb of Blue Hill) to Massapoag Lake. There, at the hotel, the riders enjoyed a dinner and dance in their cycling attire.

The following day the run was through Randolph, Braintree, Weymouth, Hingham, and to Cohasset for dinner. At Quincy, they visited the Adams House. Colonel Pope donated the refreshments for the cyclists.

Dr. Walter G. Kendall, a Boston dentist, was an early member of the Boston Bicycle Club and participated in 50 tours around the hub. On the 25th run, someone wrote the poem, "The Twenty-Fifth Time". He served as the club captain for 52 years and composed the poem, "The Men Who Ride for Fun."

The Boston Bicycle Club will always be remembered as the foremost of all the various movements of defense and development affecting the complex interests of bicyclists in this country.

The Twenty-Fifth Time

Did you know Dr. Kendall, who captains this club,
Was achieving his twenty-fifth Wheel Round the Hub?
For the fourth of a century, natives askance
Have been gazing each fall on his passionate pants.
Once we all shook our heads and went croaking like frogs,
When we heard that the Doctor had gone to the Dogs.
If we'd bet on him then we'd have surely been stung.
For he isn't dead yet. He's confoundedly young.
    For the twenty-fifth time, for the twenty-fifth time,
    Has the landlord declared he was looking sublime,
    As he hied to the washroom and cleaned off the grime,
    After Dead Ham for lunch for the twenty-fifth time.

In the camera's eye he has looked every year,
With an air of distinction, polite yet severe,
While the awed and admiring Roxbury crowd
Thought his manner inspiring, and said so out loud.
They imagined, of course, that he wallowed in riches,
As a poor man could never indulge in such breeches.
For they sparkled and twinkled and glistened and glowed,
As he walked up the walk, or he rode up the road.
    For the twenty-fifth time, for the twenty-fifth time,
    He has led from the start the competitive climb,
    For the roughest of roads he has cared not a--dime,
    As he blew up Blue Hill for the twenty-fifth time.

There's a lot of life left in the rest of us yet,
Though the bicycle certainly does make us sweat.
And we envy the furore the Doctor arouses,
With the aid of his super-spectacular trousers,
Which are fashioned of yellow, vermilion and blue,
With a streak of Hibernian green running through.
And they shed a rich glow that illumines the way,
Till the sunset in contrast looks gloomily gray.
    For the twenty-fifth time, for the twenty-fifth time,
    Has he sat down to dinner as evening bells chime,
    With a new-laundered collar and shirt white as lime,
    As he chucked in the chuck for the twenty-fifth time.

Twenty-five appears big, but it's nothing to what
Dr. Kendall will do when his eye-teeth are cut.
And in twenty-five years we shall see him again,
Still a boy in his years, among elderly men,
With his nether integuments bright as the sun,
Riding round on his wheel in the year Forty-one.
    For the fiftieth time, for the fiftieth time,
    With the look of a man who is right in his prime.
    May I be here myself to contribute a rhyme.
    As he limbers his limbs for the fiftieth time.

ANONYMOUS

NEW YORK'S LATEST FAD—THE MICHAUX 'CYCLE CLUB
Drawn by T. De Thulstrup

The Story of the Michaux Club
Compiled from a story in *Harper's Weekly*, May 18, 1895,

The Michaux Cycle Club was New York's latest fad in 1895. It was organized as the first purely social club in existence, and it is doubtful if any ordinary cyclist would have been welcomed by this group. Mr. Wynham Quinn, Mr. Elisha Dyer, and Mr. James B. Townsend conceived the idea of forming a club where friends and acquaintances might meet during the winter months, when bicycling on the road was no longer possible. The membership included Mrs. George Gould and Mrs. William K. Vanderbilt.

The club met Monday and Thursday afternoons and Tuesday and Friday mornings at Bowman's Hall. The Hall was large, with plenty of room for a number of bicyclists to ride at the same time. On Monday and Thursday afternoons there was music, and the riders went through formations from the cotillion and rode in and out between the chairs.

A reading room was available where new magazines could be read and tea was served. Club runs were posted with notices of stopovers at fashionable restaurants in town. There were always several cycling instructors in the hall, offering lessons and watching out for riders who had not mastered the art and might cause an accident.

Most of the ladies kept their riding attire at the club. They always presented a smart turnout. As a rule, there was no display of short skirts, and no bloomers or knickerbockers. The most satisfactory costumes were those made by a tailor, somewhat on the plan of an equestrian riding habit. A typical outfit was a tight-fitting jacket and a skirt, plain and full enough to show the trim little boots and leggings.

The Touring Club de France
This club was founded in 1890 with the object of promoting bicycle tours in France and other countries. The early membership of only 509 in 1890 increased to 24,396 in 1895. The Prince of Wales was an honorary member.

The Club headquarters was in the Bois de Boulogne. The first project was to establish a printed list of tariffs for the hotels that catered to cyclists. Road signs were posted around Paris and special cycle paths were built for safe cycling. In 1900. some 250 miles of cycle paths were opened. A permit was issued to members that served as identification when touring in foreign countries, the equivalent of a passport. The Club also arranged special rates for bicycles and riders on river steamers and railroads.

A famous Touring Club de France leader was "Velocio" (Paul de Vivie). He was an exponent of cycle touring and founder of the magazine *Le Cycliste*. For many years he organized a meeting of cycle tourists of the world, held at St. Etienne. In 1949, he led a large group of French riders who enjoyed a tour of England. They were entertained by the Cyclists' Touring Club at Harwich.

Touring Greats

Dr. Paul Dudley White
Our Pioneer for Safe Cycling Paths
"Bicycling provides pleasurable and economical transportation and recreation and promotes better physical and mental health."

Dr. White was born June 6, 1886, in Roxbury, Massachusetts. He graduated from Harvard with an M.D. in 1911, and subsequently served as a Captain of the United States Army Medical Corps in 1917. An eminent heart specialist and consultant to the late President Eisenhower, he was the founder of the American Heart Association.

His cycling career started as a youth when he rode his bicycle to the Roxbury Latin School, and later to Harvard. For over 75 years he was a cyclist, hiker and skater. In 1960 he led the Inaugural Ride along the Charles River Basin Bicycle Path. He served as the president of the Committee for Safe Bicycling.

I had the pleasure of meeting and bicycling with Dr. White at the American Youth Hostel Rally at Bantam Lake, Connecticut, in the early 1970's. The weekend tour was hosted by Bill Nelson, the hostel leader. Included in the party of 40 were Dr. Clifford L. Graves, who was to found the International Bicycle Touring Society, Otto Eisele of the Amateur Bicycle League of America, and John Auerbach of the Bicycle Institute. On the first afternoon Dr. White led the cyclists on a delightful pleasure tour around the lake. In the evening he gave an informal talk on the value of bicycling in retarding heart disease in middle-aged Americans. He devoted many years of his later life to investigating auto-bicycle accidents.

At the meeting Dr. White told me that he would gladly travel anywhere in the United States to attend the opening ceremonies of safe cycling paths. Later he did come to New York City and opened the new Alley Pond Park Cycle Path in Queens.

Dr. White will always be remembered as a friendly and unassuming man, ready to serve mankind and promote safe bicycling. He was elected unanimously to the American Bicycle Hall of Fame, and served as Honorary President during his last five years. This great friend of world bicycling died in 1975.

Stanley Cotterell
Founder of the Cyclists Touring Club of England (C.T.C.)
The C.T.C. is the largest and most powerful cycling club in the world.

The idea of a national bicycle touring club came from a young man named Stanley Cotterell. He lived in Birmingham and was a journalist and antique book dealer. Cotterell enjoyed touring England with fellow riders on his ordinary (or high-wheel), in spite of the sandy and muddy highways of the period.

In 1877 he suggested the formation of the national group in *Bicycling Times*. A meeting was held at Harrogate on August 5, 1878, where 50 riders met to organize the Bicycle Touring Club. Later the name was changed to the Cyclists Touring Club (C.T.C.)

The aims of the C.T.C. were to promote touring by bicycle, to help tourists secure companions, and to protect the members. Even after a hundred years, the aims remain the same.

Cotterell was elected the first president, and his interest in the club never faltered. When the club had a financial deficit he made up the loss from his own pocket.

The C.T.C. has set high standards for bicycle touring clubs throughout the world, including its cousin, The League of American Wheelmen.

Stanley Cotterell has been described by his friends as peace-loving, quiet, kind, generous and unassuming. He died on July 17, 1939, at the age of 81. In memory of the founder, the C.T.C. headquarters are known as Cotterell House. A special memorial plaque has been planned to honor "Founder Stanley John Ambrose Cotterell."

George Herbert Stancer (G.H.S.)
Cyclists Touring Club Leader for Over 50 Years
G.H. Stancer, Order of the British Empire, was born in 1878 in Yorkshire. He was active in all aspects of the sport. In his youth he was a man of speed; at the turn of the century he was a record breaker, and he became an authority on road records and racing men.

He was the editor of *Cycling* for ten years, and in 1920 was secretary of the Cyclists' Touring Club, of which he was president for the last 14 years of his life. Later he enjoyed tricycling and was president of the Tricycle Association.

STANLEY J. A. COTTERELL, FOUNDER OF THE CYCLISTS TOURING CLUB
From *The Winged Wheel* by William Oakley
Courtesy of the Cyclists Touring Club

As a champion of cyclists and a fighter for their rights, Mr. Stancer was unique. He was a walking encyclopedia of bicycling information.

For about twenty years I was a penpal of G.H.S. He offered valuable advice on how American bicyclists might solve the problems of bicycle taxation and highway licenses. Mrs. Stancer visited America and was the guest of honor at the Amateur Bicycle League of America; she addressed the group about her husband's contributions to world cycling. Mr. Stancer passed on in 1962.

A memorial is now under way to honor "George Herbert Stancer, Fighter for Bicyclists Rights."

Dick Swan

This English American cyclist was one of the most famous riders in the Hardly Able Run from Philadelphia to Mount Holly, New Jersey, for over a decade. The complete story of his cycling activities would fill a book.

A summary of his most famous accomplishments follow:

Author of: *Bert Harris of the Polly*, 1964
The Life and Times of Charley Barden, 1965
Days of Davies, 1968

Racing Career: Winner of over 400 races in Europe, Africa and Asia from 1933 to 1963.

Club Memberships: Life Member Polytechnic Cycling Club and Cyclists Touring Club of England, member of the Century Road Club Association of America and twenty other famous cycling clubs.

International Official: National Cyclists Union of England, The United States Cycling Federation and Bund Deutscher Radfahrer -(Ruhr) as judge, starter, referee, promoter, clerk of course, timer, etc.

Coaching: Chief Coach of the National Cyclists' Union and Captain of the Polytechnic Cycling Club of England.

Charles E. Pratt

Founder Member of the League of American Wheelmen
Of the three founding fathers of the League of American Wheelmen—Frank W. Weston, C. Kirk Monroe and Charles E. Pratt—Pratt was voted the highest honor, the presidency, which he accepted on May 31, 1880.

Charles Pratt is known for his literary accomplishments, which include the first book on cycling, entitled *The American Bicycler*, published in 1879, several poems and a song ("The Song of the Wheel"), and many magazine articles including "A Wheel Around the Hub," published in *Scribner's Monthly*, February, 1880.

For many years he was associated with the Pope Manufacturing Company. The *Bicycling World* of the period said of him, "Mr. Pratt is a jolly good fellow." Pratt was honored by being elected to the American Bicycle Hall of Fame in New York City. He was instrumental in setting the aims for the League: "to serve, to protect, and to further the rights and interests of wheelmen and to encourage and facilitate touring."

The league of American Wheelmen was born at Newport, Rhode Island on May 29-31 in 1880. There were 150 cyclists representing 32 clubs at the meet. Starting with an initial membership of 500, it grew to 102,636 in 1898. The League has done outstanding work for American cyclists. It obtained the right for all wheelmen to pedal on the streets and in the parks, and started a campaign for good roads and safe cycling paths. They promoted century runs, tours, parades, bicycle day, and an annual convention (held in a different city each year). Today the League publishes an attractive magazine, *American Wheelmen*, edited by Ms. Phyllis W. Harmon, who has been a member for several decades. During the past bicycling boom years, League membership has jumped to almost 16,000, due partly to the efficient promotional efforts of both Phyllis Harmon and Keith Kingbay of the Schwinn Bicycle Company.

In 1887, Abbot Bassett was elected secretary and editor of the Official Bulletin and Scrap Book of the League of American Wheelmen. He was one of the grand old veteran League members. He and his wife toured America on their high-wheel tricycle at the same time that the Pennell's of Philadelphia toured Europe. Bassett kept the League going until his death in 1924.

I joined the League in 1917. I was a penpal of Mr. Bassett and was asked to join the reporting staff for the New York area. Some of my published touring articles include "Tour to Washington D.C. 1920," "New York-Atlantic City-Philadelphia Run," and the "Two Flag Run" (New York to Montreal and back). Fellow club rider James C. Paul set the record from New York to Atlantic City in 1919. How well I remember the sandy road from Lakewood to Absecon which slowed down the party.

Today the League of American Wheelmen, with its young energetic leaders, is again America's leading touring organization. The headquarters is at 19 South Bothwell, Palatine, Illinois 60067.

The Story of Abbot Bassett

For over 25 years Mr. Bassett was secretary of the League of American Wheelmen and editor of the Official Bulletin and Scrap Book.

On September 27, 1883 he made the first triple century (300 miles) within 24 hours, establishing a new United

MR. AND MRS. ABBOTT BASSETT, ON THE COLUMBIA TANDEM
Mr. Bassett was secretary/editor of the League of American Wheelmen.
Courtesy of *Bicycling World* and *L.A.W. Bulletin*

States record in spite of a heavy machine and poor roads. With Mrs. Bassett he toured America on a high-wheel tricycle. As late as 1920 he toured the Adirondacks with 12 L.A.W. members and met Mr. Melvil Dewey at the Lake Placid Club.

Mr. Bassett participated in 83 long League tours, all of which were reported in the Official Bulletin. I enjoyed the honor and pleasure of working with Abbot Bassett for five years, writing about New York State touring news. Abbot Bassett died in 1924.

Monroe and Isabel Smith
Founders of the American Youth Hostels

Monroe W. Smith was born in Sunderland, Massachusetts, January 2, 1901. He received his Ph.B. degree from Wesleyan and an M.A. from Columbia University. In 1924 he married Isabel Bacheler, his life partner in the new youth movement. They were blessed with three children, all outdoor enthusiasts.

After graduating from college, the couple toured Europe on bicycles. While in Germany they met with Richard Schirrman, a German school teacher who organized many school and college youth tours afoot and awheel. He arranged low-cost overnight housing for these "wander tours" in old castles, inns and farm houses. The idea appealed to the Smiths, who organized the American Youth Hostels headquartered at Northfield, Massachusetts. The first hostel was established at Northfield in 1934. President and Mrs. Franklin D. Roosevelt were honorary presidents. The hostel idea was an immediate success.

In 1929, I enjoyed a summer session course at the University of Vienna in Austria. The course title was "The New Youth Movement in Europe"; it outlined the projected world youth hosteling idea. After a visit with the Smiths at Northfield, I joined the American Youth Hostels and established hostel clubs in four New York high schools. The New York City Board of Education showed slight interest in the project, because it apparently was interested only in sport activities that would bring in profits from athletic competitions.

The Smiths have been elected to the American Bicycle Hall of Fame and are listed in "Who's Who."

There are over 100,000 hostelers in the United States today; the world membership is over 3,000,000. The United States has more than 200 hostels. The federal government has allocated funds for the movement. Hostelers conserve fuel, never pollute the air, and deserve every encouragement possible. Hosteling started with cycling, but today includes hiking, mountaineering, sailing, horseback riding and camping. Hostelers use public transportation only when necessary. Today adult trips are also available, though some European hostels have a 25-year age limit.

The 1978 A.Y.H. "High Road to Adventure" lists these world trips: United States, Canada, Europe, Asia, and Australia. Remember the slogan, "IT'S FUN TO KEEP FIT BY HOSTELING!"

Dr. Clifford Graves
Founder of the International Bicycle Touring Society
Bicycle touring is a way of life with Dr. Graves, founder and leader of this 600 adult-member group . He began his cycling career when he was a medical officer in the United States Army Medical Corps in World War II.

On his return to California he kept up his keen interest in bicycle touring. His touring program included his native California, New England, France, England and Japan. In France he met the Nogretts, a tandem couple who guided him through interesting places in France. Dr. Graves reciprocated by showing them the United States awheel.

I had the pleasure of meeting Dr. Graves on a weekend cycling tour to Bantam Lake in Connecticut. The late Dr. Paul Dudley White acted as tour pacemaker. We stopped at the American Youth Hostel for an evening of cycle touring talks and sociability.

This meeting resulted in the birth of the International Bicycle Touring Society. Under the expert leadership of Dr. Graves, the society had a tremendous growth. It appeals to the over-40 age group. All tours are planned in

31

advance and there is no need to carry a pup tent, sleeping bag, or cooking utensils. Meals are enjoyed at specified restaurants, and overnights spent at comfortable motels and tourist homes.

The 1978 schedule included England, France, Austria and all sections of the United States including Hawaii. All the tours are led by experienced leaders. Dr. Graves tells his touring story in a new book entitled *Sportsources*.

Information on tours is available from the International Bicycle Touring Society at 846 Prospect, La Jolla, California 92037.

Roland C. Geist
The Bicycle Touring League of America

I began my cycling career in 1899 riding on the handlebars of my father's new Columbia bicycle. My first tour was from my home in Harlem, New York to Coney Island, a distance of about 20 miles. I still remember passing the huge Fifth Avenue stage coaches, the big reservoir at 42nd Street, the Brooklyn Bridge, and the thousands of cyclists riding on the tree-shaded Coney Island Cycle Path.

My 1902 Christmas present was a new Crescent bicycle equipped with a new Departure coaster brake. Escorted by my uncle and friends, I enjoyed tours to the Delaware Water Gap, Southampton (my first century thrill), New Haven and Asbury Park. In 1919 as captain of the Century Road Club Association of New York, I led summer vacation tours to Boston, Montreal, Toronto and Albany. All of the club members rode fixed gear racing machines; gear shifts were unheard of.

In 1936, the New Haven Railroad started operating weekend cycle trains to the Berkshires. I met some interesting cycling companions on the train, all college people. We decided to meet every Sunday to enjoy these grand outings away from the city motor traffic. We organized an informal group without dues and fees known as the College Cycle Club. The voluntary leaders included president Thea Stephan, M.A. (Columbia), and secretary Roland C. Geist, J.D. (New York University).

About 1950, the group decided to change its name to the Bicycle Touring League of America, and to invite any person interested in bicycle touring to join us. The policy of no dues or fees was continued. The secretary sent out postcard notices of coming events.

The League secretary planned and led a series of tours. In 1952, a weekend Cape Cod tour via the Colonial Line from New York to New Bedford with scenic cycling to Woods Hole and return via steamer; a Hudson River Day Line tour by steamer to Poughkeepsie, cycling down alongside the river road to Bear Mountain and then back on the steamer; a week-long tour to Nantucket and Martha's Vineyard starting from New Bedford via steam-

er to the quiet island havens. On Nantucket the Dr. Paul Dudly White cycle path had just been opened and twelve members of the St. Louis Cycling Club joined us. A wealthy resident of the island invited the whole party to a motorboat tour around Nantucket - a real treat. In 1971, a party of 40 made the Austro-American Good Will Cycle Tour, cycling from Graz to Vienna with side trips to Yugoslavia and some points of historical interest. There were also auto-camping-cycling tours to the national parks, including Arcadia in Maine, Shenandoah in Virginia, Grand Canyon in Arizona, Yosemite in California, Yellowstone in Wyoming and Glacier in Montana. In the Grand Teton National Park we met a Mr. Owen, who was about 80 years of age and the first man to pedal around Yellowstone National Park on a high-wheel. His bicycle is on exhibit in the Madison Museum.

Most of the early League members, now in their 70's or older, still enjoy each other's company. Members and friends still meet at the annual New York City events: the International Cycle Show, the Pepsi Bicycle Marathon in Central Park, and the New York Bicycle Banquet and Old Home Day at the American Bicycle Hall of Fame in Richmondtown on Staten Island, New York.

Robert E. McNair
Founder of The Wheelman

In 1967, Robert McNair of Swarthmore, Pennsylvania conceived the idea of collecting antique bicycles, restoring them and riding them in parades, fairs and tours. He served as The Wheelmen's first national commander and established an active organization of over 600 members. For many years, he led The Wheelmen in diverse interesting activities. He was recently elected Commander Emeritus.

Over the years, the members have enjoyed riding their ordinaries in the annual Mummers parade held on New Years Day in Philadelphia, in the Macy Thanksgiving Day parade in New York, and at the Old Home Day ceremonies at the American Bicycle Hall of Fame on the Richmondtown Restoration in New York City. A few years ago the group held its annual reunion at the home and museum of fellow member Roger Johnson at Hadley, Massachusetts. Johnson has a large antique bicycle collection; many of the models were in rideable condition, and members rode them around his estate.

Under the leadership of Bob McNair the club started publishing *The Wheelmen*. This fascinating magazine prints well-researched articles and old photos of bicycling in the earlier days. Members also receive a newsletter which is "Dedicated to the Enjoyment and Preservation of our Bicycling Heritage." Associate Editor Irving A. Leonard of The Wheelmen has published a unique book entitled *When Bikehood Was in Flower*.

The writer feels honored to be an early member of The Wheelmen.

Annual Bicycle Tours

Henry Hope Reed
Organizer of the Friends of the Parks in New York City
Henry Reed is the Curator of Central Park, and with his many friends in every station of life has organized bicycling and hiking tours for New Yorkers. On these tours they visit places of historic and natural interest. The public is invited to join on payment of a small fee which goes to the preservation of trees in parks.

A few years ago I participated in a middle-of-the-night bicycle tour. About a hundred riders met in midtown at 2 a.m. on a Sunday and rode up to Pelham Bay Park, where we enjoyed a picnic breakfast. Our return trip to Times Square was via a special subway train

On August 28, 1977 a most unusual Insomniac Bicycle Tour was held from New York to Washington, D.C., At 8 p.m. on a Saturday night over a hundred cyclists met at Penn Station and boarded a special Amtrak train for Union Station in Washington. Arriving about 3 a.m. the riders met their leaders, including Mrs. Elizabeth Moynihan, wife of the senator from New York, Henry Hope Reed, and Michael George. Some riders had joined the party in Philadelphia and many more joined in Washington. A party of several hundred rode the 19 ½ mile route around the capital. The group pedalled along the famous Rock Creek Park cycle path and, of course, all around the famous buildings. As the sun rose, the cyclists rested by the pool at the Jefferson Memorial. Members of the party ranged in age from 11 to over 60 years. The special round trip train rate was only $33.00.

(Some bystanders remarked that the idea was a form of lunacy.) For further information on both biking and hiking tours write:

Friends of Central Park
Lenox Hill P.O. Box 610
New York, N Y 10021

The Atlantic City Bicycle Festival
For many years the Visitors Bureau of Atlantic City sponsored an annual Bicycle Festival. It was often held in August before the Miss America Contest. I am told that in the early days of the big pageant the contestants had to pedal along the boardwalk as one of their talents.

At the 1952 Festival over a hundred byclists dressed in fancy attire rode before the judges at the Convention Hall

to compete for trophies. The parade started with veterans riding the high-wheels in their 1880 cycling costumes.

Three trophies were awarded, "Miss Bicycle of America," "Mr. and Mrs. Bicycle of America," and "Mr. Bicycle of America." I was astonished to be awarded the "Mr. Bicycle" Trophy. It is a cherished prize and still stands on top of my bookcase.

Since 1976 Atlantic City has been the site of the Pro-Am Bike Race that attracts thousands to the resort each September. President Katherine Cramer has done a tremendous job of making this event an outstanding race in American cycling history.

New York City Five-Borough Bicycle Marathon
3,000 See New York City by Pedal Power
Sunday, April 30, 1978 was a grand day for cycling. To veterans it brought back memories of the Gay Nineties when bicycling was a way of life.

The New York American Youth Hostel clubs and the Board of Education planned this five-borough marathon, open to all for a $1.00 registration fee. A school bus known as a "Sag Wagon" picked up the stragglers en route.

The 35-mile route started from the Manhattan City Hall at 7 a.m. and continued via the Brooklyn Bridge along the Brooklyn-Queens Expressway. Police squad cars cleared the highways for the riders, which made it both safe and delightful. After a short stop in the Bronx, the cyclists continued via the F.D.R. Drive to the Battery for lunch. Music was provided by hostelers playing kazoos and guitars. After a two-hour lunch the cyclists enjoyed a boat ride to St. George, Staten Island. Subways permitted the riders and bicycles to get home the easy way.

Mayor Koch and City Council President Carol Bellamy joined the happy riders for a few miles. Stephen Bauman of the American Youth Hostels described the marathon as affording fantastic views of the Manhattan skyline and the bay from the base of the Verrazano Bridge: "It's amazing how beautiful the streets around are, as seen from a slow-moving bicycle."

For a day New York City was turned into a Pedaler's Paradise. All cyclists are cordially invited to join future City Bicycle Marathons.

Old Home Day Tour to the American Bicycle Hall of Fame
This annual tour, parade and exhibition is held the third Sunday of each October, weather permitting. It is sponsored by the Bicycle Touring League of America and the Antique Bicycle Club of America. It is a non-profit and non-commercial event. Those who do not come on

**ATLANTIC CITY BICYCLE FESTIVAL
1952**

bicycles are asked to contribute a dollar toward keeping up the Hall of Fame Museum.

The cyclists usually meet at 10 a.m. at South Ferry, Manhattan. The route is via *"Bikeway"* signs to Richmond, Staten Island, a distance of 8 miles.

The activities of Old Home Day include:

1. A parade at about noon from the parking lot with antique autos, people dressed in colonial attire, hobby clubs, hiking groups, etc.
2. About 1 p.m. in the parking lot there are exhibitions by invited clubs on high-wheels (The Wheelmen), the unicyclists (The Unicyclists Association of America) and others.
3. A visit to the antique bicycle collection at the Historical Museum.
4. A meeting of the Board of Governors of the American Bicycle Hall of Fame to elect a famous cyclist to be

enshrined in the Hall. (Seventeen have been elected in the past twenty years.)

The American Bicycle Hall of Fame is one of the 20 old colonial buildings of the restoration open to the public at Richmond. The Curator was Loring McMillen of the Staten Island Historical Society.

The antique bicycle collection dates back to 1869. The latest addition is the 32-foot-high unicycle donated by Steve McPeak and Bill Jenack of the Unicyclists Association of America. All bicyclists and friends are welcome.

Arthur Vickery and Tom Lockhart
The Hardly Able Run From Philadephia to Mount Holly, New Jersey

The Hardly Able Run is the oldest semi-annual bicycle pleasure tour still active in America. It was started about the turn of the century by veteran riders Vickery and Lockhart of the Century Road Club of America. Today the Hill Cycle Shop promotes the event.

The odd name was conceived during a rest stop; when some old time riders wondered if in years to come they would be able to finish the run. It is a go-as-you-please event of about 50 miles round trip through scenic New Jersey countryside. In the beginning the party numbered about 35. Today over 500 join in this unique pleasure tour.

In the 1930's, the leading pacemakers included Louis Knauth of the Cycling Enthusiasts, Ed Bates of the Pennsylvania Bicycle Club, Fred Kuhn of the Century Road Club of America, the Delong tandem team from the League of American Wheelmen, and cameraman Al Hatos, along with me and many other enthusiasts.

The route lay from the Tacony Palmyra Bridge to Mount Holly, New Jersey via the Quaker settlement of Moorestown. At Mount Holly the groups enjoyed a picnic lunch. Some of the men and women who rode in the twenties still attend today, but they arrive by auto. At Hack's Canoe Rest at Mount Holly, canoes may be rented and impromptu canoe competitions are held by two-man teams from the participating clubs.

Short Annual Tours

Bicycle leaders in other cities have also conducted one and two day pleasure tours.

One of the more popular is "Tour of the Scioto River Valley" (known as the TSRV). It is a 210-mile two-day tour round trip from Columbus, Ohio to Portsmouth, Ohio under the direction of the American Youth Hostels. A Bicycle Marathon is held at Belle Isle, Detroit, Michigan.

In Chicago, Boston, Philadelphia, Washington, and many other cities, American Youth Hostel leaders provide one-day tours for cycling enthusiasts.

Cycle Trains

The Popular Cycle Trains from New York City

In 1936, the New Haven Railroad operated delightful one-day excursions for bicyclists, hikers, camera fans and foldboaters to the Berkshires and the Housatonic River Valley areas. Over 400 bicycles were available for rental from Ben Olken of Cambridge, Massachusetts. These trains left Grand Central at 8 a.m. and carried the happy riders to Falls Village, West Cornwall, Kent, and other neighboring towns, and returned to New York City at 9 p.m. It was a safe and wonderful day in the country.

The foldboaters paddled their boats down the white waters of the Housatonic River; it was a real thrill with many spills. We cyclists often stood on the bridges and watched the daring young men navigate the treacherous white waters.

The last New York Cycle Train went out just before World War II with over 900 enthusiasts aboard. I will always remember the many friends I met on the train and on the side roads en route to Lake Buel.

The New Haven Lines also operated a Picture Cycle Train from Boston. The train left South Station at 7 a.m. and took the riders to Woods Hole, where the steamer brought the party to Oak Bluffs on Martha's Vineyard. The cyclists made delightful short trips to quaint fishing villages on the island. The Ocean House at Nantucket, which was the next stop on the tour, offered a special cyclists' luncheon for only $1.00.

Chicago cyclists also formed cycle trains to places of scenic interest in their area.

The Jersey Central and Long Island Railroad Cycle Trains

The Jersey Central Lines operated Sunday Cycle Trips starting in the 1940's. They advertised "Fun, Frolic, Health, Exercise and Fresh Air" to everyone. Tours were offered from April to November at low rates ranging from $2.50 to $3.50 round trip.

The cycling destinations included Lakewood, Atlantic Highlands, Raritan, Bound Brook, Red Bank, and a Mystery Trip (information on train).

About 1966 the Metropolitan Council of the American Youth Hostels sponsored Long Island Railroad cycle trains to the Hamptons. I enjoyed the 1966 tour with over 600 hostelers of all ages. These trips were all on level terrain but there were headwinds to face. A happy but tired crowd returned to Pennsylvania Station at 9 p.m.

I find that every cycle train offers a glorious adventure awheel.

**FIRST AUSTRO-AMERICAN GOOD WILL
TOUR 1971**

Courtesy of the Minister of Tourism and Sport of Styria

Special Tours
1939 AND 1940

Bicycles at the New York World's Fair of 1939 and 1940

The first Bicycle Day at the New York World's Fair was held Sunday June 11, 1939. Several hundred cyclists met at Columbus Circle, wearing colorful attire for the short run to the Flushing Meadows fair grounds. Free admission was granted to all who arrived on bicycles.

At the Fair the riders assembled at the Cycle Trades of America Pavillion, where they met the world-famous "Mile-a-Minute Murphy." He told stories of his great ride and signed autographs. The salon was decorated with colorful flags and cycling photos.Many bicycles were on display at the French, English and Belgian buildings. At the English Hall of Sports, the original McMillen bicycle of 1839 was on exhibit.

In the evening the riders enjoyed a performance of the American Jubilee, a colorful historical bicycle ballet staged by Albert Johnson with music by Oscar Hammerstein II and Arthur Schwartz. The hit of the bicycle ballet was the song entitled "My Bicycle Girl," published by Chappell and Company of New York.

Joe Jackson offered his "Tramp Cyclist" comedy act and the Gay Nineties tandem couple of Blair and Christie portrayed Lillian Russell and Diamond Jim Brady. At the Chase and Sanborn pavillion the famous puppeteer Sue Hastings presented Mr. Chase and Mr. Sanborn riding a tandem.

I saw the American Jubilee three times and still have pleasant memories of the catchy tunes, the artistic bicycle ballet riding and the scenic sets.

1971

First Austro-American Good Will Bicycle Tour

The Austro-American Tour trip started from Graz, with a warm welcome from Josef Krainer, Governor of Styria. Mayor Charles F. Horn, of Ketterling, Ohio made the acceptance speech for the "American Cowboys on Bicycles."

The Puch factory provided all riders with multi-geared lightweight touring bicycles for the two-week stay. Daily tours were made from centers at Graz and Baden. Almost every evening there was a formal banquet with wine, music and dancing. En route some of the tour members made a tape for broadcasting, and near Vienna television cameras filmed the riders touring the countryside.

Daily mileage was low to allow novices to keep up with the party. Old castles, churches, caves, museums, the stud farm where the famous Lipizzaner white horses of Vienna are trained, and the hunting lodge, the scene of the Mayerling tragedy, were visited.

In Vienna the group enjoyed the opera "Tales of Hoffman," and made a tour of the Palace at Schonbrun. The National Library offered a special exhibit of old books and prints on bicycling. Old bicycle prints were on sale at the century-old shops. In the afternoon there was indoor ice skating at the Stadthalle.

Tour members represented the following national organizations: the League of American Wheelmen, the International Bicycle Touring Society, the Bicycle Touring League of America, the American Youth Hostels, the Cyclists' Touring Club of London, the Antique Bicycle Club and The Wheelmen.

Tour members were welcomed everywhere by officials and public alike. They all learned the Austrian bicycle song, "Here We Come With the Bikes," and parted singing "Auf Wiedersehen."

1976

The Bicentennial Tour

To commemorate America's Bicentennial in 1976, Dan and Lys Burden of Missoula, Montana conceived a Trans-America Bicycle Trail. The Bicycle Manufacturers Association of America donated $10,000 to the project; the United States Department of Transportation, the American Youth Hostels, and the League of American Wheelmen all cooperated in the tour plans. The trail started at Yorktown, Virginia and finished at Astoria, Oregon, crossing 10 states, 25 national forests and the Teton and Yellowstone national parks, a distance of about 4,000 miles. Interested cyclists may pedal the trail today. For information write Trans-America Bicycle Trail, P.O. Box 1034, Missoula, Montana 59801.

The Wheelmen's Bicentennial Tour

The Wheelmen's most memorable outing was the 750-mile Bicentennial Tour from Independence Hall in Greenfield Village, Michigan, to Independence Hall in Philadelphia in 1976. Twenty-six hardy high-wheel riders survived the trip. Bob Green of England, representing the Southern Veteran Cycle Club, completed the entire distance on his ten-speed bicycle.

In Philadelphia, the victorious riders were welcomed by National Commander Edwin Gerling. More than a hundred members dressed in period attire assembled in front of Independence Hall. Govenor Milliken of Michigan sent a congratulatory message to Philadelphia's Mayor Rizzo.

There were a few mechanical mishaps en route—60 broken spokes and 25 loosened tires—and some tour members had taken headers along the way, but everyone joined in the big parade. From Independence Hall the riders pedaled to Fairmount Park; it was a festive conclusion to a great event in the history of American cycling.

I first visited Independence Hall in 1915 on a bicycle tour from New York to Atlantic City to Philadelphia under the auspices of the Century Road Club Association of New York and the Quaker City Wheelmen. On the hot July Sunday of 1976 during the Bicentennial Tour it was a pleasure to meet old cycling friends and renew friendships of yesteryear.

THE CYCLISTS, 1897
By Jay Hambridge

ANNUALLY

The East Coast Bicycle Trail

Tom Pendelton, who represents the American Youth
Hostels and the Federal Department of Transportation
founded The East Coast Bicycle Trail. It stretches 1,000
miles from Boston, Massachusetts to Richmond, Virginia
by-passing the big-city traffic. A trail extension is being
considered to Georgia and to Montreal. This is an
opportunity for those who did not wish to pedal the 4,000
Trans-America Trail to enjoy a week or two on the new
East Coast Bicycle Trail. For further information write
to:

East Coast Bicycle Congress
626 South 4th Street
Philadelphia, Pa. 19147

Bicycle Touring Bibliography

Allen, T.G. and Sachtleben, *Across Asia on a Bicycle*,
Century, New York, 1894.
Asa, Warren, *North American Bicycle Atlas*, Hammond,
New York.

Bauer, Fred, *How Many Hills to Hillsboro,* Hewitt, Tappan, N.Y., 1969.

Baron, Stanley, *Westward Ho,* Jarrolds, London, 1944.

Birchmore, Fred, *Around the World on a Bicycle,* University of Georgia Press, 1939.

Burston and Stokes, *Round the World on Bicycles,* Robertson, Melbourne, 1890.

Callan, Hugh, *From the Clyde to the Jordan,* Blackie, London, 1895.

Cavan, Earl of, *With the Yacht, Camera and Cycle in the Mediterranean,* Sampson, Low and Co. London, 1895.

Davar, F.J., *Cycling Over the Roof of the World,* Zeidler, New York, 1929.

Duthie, James, *I Cycled into the Arctic Circle,* Stockwell, Ilfracombe, 1955.

Elvin, Harold, *The Ride to Chandigarh,* Macmillan, London, 1957.

Fraser, John Foster, *Round the World on a Wheel,* Methuen, London, 1905.

Garrison, W.W., *Wheeling Through Europe,* Christian Pub. Company, St. Louis, 1900.

Golden, S., *A Tandem Tour in Norway,* Iliffe and Son, London, 1888.

Grivell, H., *Australian Cycling in the Golden Days,* Currier Unley, 1952.

Hakim, Bapsola and Bhumgara, *With the Cyclists Round the World,* Captain Press, Bombay, 1928.

Hamann, Walter, *Mit Dem Fahrrad Um Die Welt,* Schneider, Munchen, 1967.

Hamsher, W. Papel, *The Balkans by Bicycle,* Witherby, London, 1917.

Hawkins, Gary and Karen, *Bicycle Touring in Europe,* Pantheon, New York, 1973.

Helfgen, Heinz, *Ich Radle um Die Welt,* H. Fischer Bielefeld, 1955.

Jefferson, Robert L., *A New Ride to Khiva,* Methuen, London, 1899.

Jefferson, Robert L., *Awheel to Moscow and Back,* Sampson Low, London, 1895.

King, Arthur, *Awheel to the Artic Circle,* Fowler, London, 1940.

Leonard, Irving, *First Across America by Bicycle,* Private Printing, 1965.

Murphy, Claude C., *Around the U.S. by Bicycle,* Taylor, Detroit, 1906.

Newman, Bernard, *Ride to Russia,* Jenkins, London, 1938.

Newman, Bernard, *Ride to Rome,* Jenkins, London, 1953.

Pennell, Joseph and Elizabeth Robbins, *Over the Alps on a Bicycle,* T. Fisher Unwin, London, 1898.

Pennell, Joseph and Elizabeth Robbins, *Our Sentimental Journey Through France and Italy,* T. Fisher Unwin, London, 1893.

Pennell, Joseph and Elizabeth Robbins, *Two Pilgrims Progress,* Little Brown, Boston, 1899.

Pohl, Roderick, *Mit dem Fahrrad Nach Kalkutta,* Wuppetal, 1968.

Stevens, Thomas, *Around the World on a Bicycle,* Scribners, N.Y., 1887 (Two Volumes).

Thorenfeldt, Kai, *Round the World on a Cycle,* Selwyn and Blount, London 1928

Tilman, H.W., *Snow on the Equator,* Macmillan, New York, 1938.

Wellbye, Reginald, *Cycle Touring at Home and Abroad,* Temple, London, 1890.

Wray, W. Fitzwater, *Across France in War Time,* J.M. Dent, London, 1916.

THE FIRST BICYCLE RACE 1869

The winner was James Moore (right) of England.

40

3
THE RACERS

THE CURRENT BICYCLING BOOM HAS brought a renewed interest in racing. This chapter presents highlights of the famous racers and racing events of the world.

The first road race was held on November 17, 1869 on boneshakers from Paris to Rouen. It was won by James Moore of Great Britain. In 1880 a high-wheel bicycle track race was held in New York City.

Bicycle racing may be classified as amateur or professional. Amateurs may not receive a cash prize for winning. However, an American amateur cyclist may receive a small cash prize in races called "Pro-Am" races.

Racing is also classified as road or track. Different types of bicycles are used in each event. The Olympic Games offer both road and track events. Women have not yet been admitted to Olympic cycling races.

There are many types of road races, such as the criterium, the time trial, the stage race, the cyclo-cross, etc. Track racing also comes in several types, including the match sprint, the pursuit and the motor pace.

For readers interested in training, there is an informative volume on both road and track entitled *Winning Bicycle Racing*, written by Jack Simes with Barbara George. Jack Simes is a multiple National Champion racer and United States team coach. Barbara George is the publisher of a racing newspaper, *Velo-news*.

World Speed Record Holders

Story of Mile-a-Minute Murphy

Charles M. Murphy of New York was born in 1871. He was blessed with powerful arms and legs—a natural cyclist. In his prime he held the following records: seven World, seventeen United States and nine New York State titles.

After retiring from ordinary bicycle races, he conceived the idea of racing a steam locomotive. On June 30, 1899 he achieved his goal by riding behind a Long Island Railroad steam locomotive, equipped with a special shed-like shield to cut down wind resistance. Murphy covered the mile in 57.8 seconds and amazed the sporting world with this feat of speed and strength based upon the new science of streamlining.

Shortly after this speed record, Murphy joined the New York Police Department as a bicycle patrolman. His chief duties were to chase scorchers (bicyclists exceeding the eight mile an hour speed limit) and to stop runaway horses and carriages. Later he transferred to the motorcycle squad. His new duties caused him many injuries; he retired in 1917.

I met him at the the 1939 New York World's Fair. After a most interesting account of his cycling life, he gave me an autographed copy of *A Story of the Railroad and a Bicycle* in exchange for my book *Bicycling as a Hobby*. In 1960 Mr. Murphy was elected to the American Bicycle Hall of Fame.

BRUCE SMALL   H. OPPERMAN
24 HOURS. WORLD RECORD
VELODROME of MELBOURNE

Facing page:
CHARLES M. (MILE-A-MINUTE) MURPHY
June 30, 1889—One mile in 57.8 seconds. Murphy was a World Paced Speed Record holder.
Courtesy of Secretary John Auerbach and Jim Hayes of the Bicycle Institute of America

This page
Top:
SIR HUMBERT OPPERMAN OF AUSTRALIA
Holder of the 24-hour Paced Record of 860 miles, 367 yards, 1932.
Courtesy of Dick Swan

Above:
ALFRED LETOURNEUR ESTABLISHING THE WORLD BICYCLE SPEED RECORD 1941
Photo by Harry Hertz
He is also a holder of the World Paced Speed Record.

At right:
ALLAN ABBOTT, M.D., THE FASTEST BICYCLE RIDER IN THE WORLD
Dr. Abbott standing alongside his record-breaking machine. Note that the front part of the bicycle was custom-made for this event. He is a World Paced Speed Record Holder.
Courtesy of Dr. Allan Abbott

THE 25-MILE BICYCLE RACE AT THE AMERICAN INSTITUTE FAIR BUILDING
New York City, February 4, 1880

Murphy's record has been broken several times. The latest speed recorded was 138.6 miles per hour, set by Allan Abbott on August 25, 1973 on the Bonneville Salt Flats of Utah.

Death came to Mile-a-Minute Murphy on February 17, 1950 at the ripe old age of 79. He was one of the first to prove the value of streamlining to the world of science.

Alfred Letourneur

This famous French racer's story has been given in detail in the section on Six Day Racing.

Letourneur also held the world speed record for a mile, which he made pacing in back of an auto. The bicycle he used was a custom-made motor-paced machine designed with his help by the engineers of the Arnold Schwinn Company of Chicago. It had a 28-inch diameter wheel in the rear and a 24-inch diameter wheel in front. The gearing was 252, and it weighed 26.5 pounds. It was equipped with Pye racing tires inflated to 100 pounds pressure. The midget pace auto driven by Ronnie Householder was equipped with a shield to cut down wind resistance.

The American Automobile Association granted Letourneur a certificate of performance for his May 17, 1941 run made over a mile course at the Bakersfield, California track. His speed was 108.92 miles an hour.

Allan Abbott M.D.
The Fastest Bicycle Rider in the World

Dr. Abbott, 29, of San Bernadino, California established a world record on a bicycle with a speed of 138.674 miles an hour. This astounding accomplishment was made on August 25, 1973 behind a windshield mounted at the rear of an automobile, over a ¾ mile course on the Bonneville Salt Flats of Utah.

44

Dr. Allan Abbott also recorded an official unpaced 9.22 seconds for 200 meters (48.62 miles an hour) at Ontario, California on April 30, 1977.

A cash prize has been offered to anyone who can beat these great records.

Sir Hubert Opperman

This greatest of long-distance cyclists has contributed many records to the cycling sport.

Sir Hubert started his cycling career in Melbourne, Australia in the 1920's. In 1928 he won the Bol d'Or, a 24-hour-paced race on the famous Parc des Princes velodrome in Paris. Next he won the tough English "Land's End to John O'Groats." In 1932 he won the World's 24 Hour Paced Race behind a motorcycle, covering over 860 miles. This record still stands, according to the Guinness Book of World Records.

After his incredible cycling career he entered the political arena. He was elected a Member of Parliament from Australia and was named Minister and High Commisioner for Malta. His fascinating life story may be read in his book, *Pedals, Politics and People* published by Haldance Proprietory Ltd. of Australia.

World's Paced Bicycle Speed Records

Date Record Holder	Country	Track or Road	Distance and Time	
1897 Maur Lombard	F	Parc des Princes	1 K	59 1/5
1908 Will T. Hall	G.B.	Parc des Princes	1 K	40
1906 Paul Guignard	F	Munich	1 K	37 3/5
1899 Charles Murphy	U.S.A.	Long Island	1 Mile	57 4/5
1928 Leon Vanderstuyft	B	Montlhery	2.5 K	1.11.4
1931 Al Blanc-Garin	F	Montlhery	2.5 K	1.10.2
1937 Geo. Paillard	F	Montlhery	2.5 K	1.05.5
1950 Jose Meiffret	F	Grenzlandrg	1 K	25.8
1938 Alf Letourneur	F	Montlhery	2.5 K	1.01.2
1950 Karl Heinz Kramer	D	Grenzlandrg	1 K	23.30
1941 Alf Letourneur	F	Bakersfield, U.S.A.	1 K	20.53
1951 Jose Meiffret	F	Toulouse	1 K	20.50
1961 Jose Meiffret	F	Lahr	1 K	20.396
1961 Jose Meiffret	F	Lahr	1 K	20.390
1961 Jose Meiffret	F	Lahr	1 K	20.120
1962 Jose Meiffret	F	Fribourg	1 K	17.580
1973 Allan Abbott	U.S.A.	Bonneville Salt Flats, U.S.A.	1 Mile	25.960

American World Sprint Champions

A. A. Zimmerman

Arthur Augustus Zimmerman was born in Camden, New Jersey, July 11, 1869.

He began his racing career on a Star bicycle. In 1892 he toured Europe, racing in England, Germany and France. The following year he won the championships of both England and America. "The Flying Yankee," as he was called, possessed a style of riding that was easy, graceful and swift. In 1896 he visited Australia and returned with victories.

"Cycling has never seen or will see his like again," wrote reporter Victor Breyer, who saw him race and visited him in America. Zimmerman retired in the 1930's to his home near Asbury Park, New Jersey. He wrote *Zimmerman Abroad* and *Points on Training*. In addition he designed a bicycle called "The Zimmy."

Zimmerman died of a heart attack in 1936. I called on Mrs. Zimmerman in 1937 in Asbury Park and was shown a room with glass cabinets containing the many trophies and medals won by her late husband. Zimmerman was the first rider to be elected to the American Bicycle Hall of Fame.

"Major" Taylor

Marshall Walter Taylor was the only black to reach the world championship class. He was born in Indianapolis, Indiana on November 25, 1878.

He began his great cycling career as a bicycle errand boy. His debut as a professional rider came in 1896 when he competed in the New York Madison Square Garden continuous individual six day race. He lost that race but was determined to train and compete in cycle racing.

Taylor soon was competing and winning against the champions Eddie Bald, Tom Cooper and Frank Kramer. He won the national championships on an Iver Johnson bicycle given him by the company. In 1899 he competed in Montreal and won the world's title. At the Parc des Princes velodrome in Paris he defeated the great French champion Jacquelin two out of three heats and won the acclaim of France. His career shows 159 wins out of 180 starts, a remarkable record. The "Black Wonder," as he was called, retired in the 1920's. He suffered a severe head injury while competing in a race at Ipswich.

Major Taylor was a model youth, modest and clean-living. His religious beliefs prevented him from racing on Sundays. In 1928 he published the story of his life, entitled *The Fastest Bicycle Rider in the World.*

MAJOR TAYLOR, USA WORLD SPRINT CHAMPION IN 1899
Courtesy of the Staten Island Historical Society and the American Bicycle Hall of Fame

FRANK KRAMER U.S.A. WORLD
SPRINT CHAMPION IN 1912
Photo by Al Hatos

This greatest black champion of all time died July 7, 1930. He is enshrined in the American Bicycle Hall of Fame.

Frank Kramer

"Big Steve," as he was called, was born November 21, 1880 in Evansville, Indiana. His family moved to East Orange, New Jersey, where he started his racing career in 1896.

Kramer won his first national championship in 1898. From 1901 to 1916 he held the professional championship of America. Then he lost it to Spencer, but he regained it in 1918 and again in 1921. In 1905 he competed in Europe, where he won 16 races and lost only three. The French people cheered him on to win the Grand Prix of Paris in 1905 and 1906. His greatest triumph was winning the world's championship in 1912 at Newark.

He established a record for longevity, with an active racing career for over 27 years. He competed in six-day races in New York but he won only in 1912 in Boston and Newark. His interest in bicycling was life-long. He was an official in the National Cycling Association and coached youths in the grand sport. Racing editor Otto Eisele of the American Bicyclist, called him "Cyclist Extra Ordinare."

"Big Steve" died in 1958. He was elected to the American Bicycle Hall of Fame.

A.A. ZIMMERMAN U.S.A. WORLD
SPRINT CHAMPION IN 1892
Courtesy of A.A. Zimmerman

THE RALEIGH

2,300 PRIZES
UNPARALLELED LIST of RIDERS
WHO HAVE BECOME CHAMPIONS DURING 1892
L. CANTU, CHAMPION of ITALY.
A. RUSCELLI CHAMPION DES JUNIORS of ITALY.
A. GERICKE, CHAMPION of AUSTRIA,
W. FRIEDRICH CHAMPION .... of AUSTRIA
J.D. CELLIERS, CHAMPION of SOUTH AFRICA.
S. LENTON CHAMPION 150 MILES of WALES.
AND

A.A. ZIMMERMAN, N.Y.A.C.
CHAMPION OF THE WORLD
AGENCE GÉNÉRALE 76, AVENUE DES TERNES
PARIS

TOUR DE FRANCE 1955
Charley Gaul leading on Telegraph Pass.
Courtesy of United Press International

ROUTE OF TOUR DE FRANCE 1967

Courtesy *Lo Sport Illustrado*

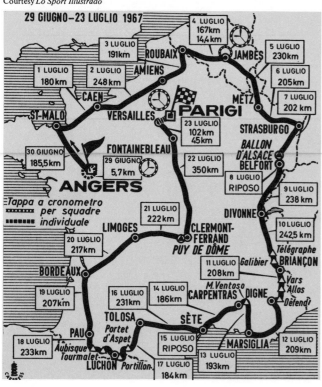

29 GIUGNO – 23 LUGLIO 1967

4 LUGLIO 167km 144 km
3 LUGLIO 191km
ROUBAIX
JAMBES
5 LUGLIO 230km
1 LUGLIO 180km
2 LUGLIO 248km
AMIENS
6 LUGLIO 205km
CAEN
METZ
7 LUGLIO 202km
ST-MALO
VERSAILLES
PARIGI
23 LUGLIO 102km 45km
STRASBURGO
BALLON D'ALSACE BELFORT
30 GIUGNO 185,5km
FONTAINEBLEAU
29 GIUGNO 5,7km
22 LUGLIO 350km
8 LUGLIO RIPOSO
ANGERS
9 LUGLIO 238km
Tappa a cronometro per squadre individuale
21 LUGLIO 222km
DIVONNE
10 LUGLIO 242,5 km
LIMOGES
CLERMONT-FERRAND PUY DE DÔME
Télégraphe BRIANÇON
20 LUGLIO 217km
11 LUGLIO Galibier 208km
Vars Allos
BORDEAUX
M.Ventoso
Defend
19 LUGLIO 207km
16 LUGLIO 231km
14 LUGLIO 186km
CARPENTRAS
DIGNE
TOLOSA
SÈTE
PAU
Portet d'Aspet
15 LUGLIO RIPOSO
MARSIGLIA
12 LUGLIO 209km
18 LUGLIO 233km
Aubisque Tourmalet
13 LUGLIO 193km
LUCHON Portillon
17 LUGLIO 184km

The Greatest Bicycle Race in the World

The Tour de France Story

This annual cross-country race, first held in 1903, is the world's outstanding cycling event.

The route runs for about 2,500 miles on the highways around the perimeter of France. The event usually starts in the northern part of France in June and finishes in Paris on Bastille Day. "The Tour," as it is known, is conducted in stages of 100 to 200 miles a day. The route is changed each year, but always crosses some high Alpine passes.

Only the expert racing cyclists of Europe compete in this grueling event. The competitors ride down the mountains at speeds from 50 to 60 miles an hour around hairpin curves. The cyclist who is first on the mountain stages is granted permission to wear a special jersey and is crowned "King of the Mountain." The tour winner receives several thousand francs and thus achieves both wealth and fame.

48

Among the great winners of modern times are Jacques Anquetil of France and Eddy Merckx of Belgium, who have each won five races. Another great European rider who won several races is Fausto Coppi of Italy. Raymond Poulidor of France won seven second and third places.

No American or Englishman has yet won a place in this big event. Tom Simpson of Great Britain did win some stages in the race but died later of exhaustion. An American team is expected to compete in this international event in a year or so.

Other classic long distance races in Europe include tours of Belgium, Italy, Netherlands, Spain and Switzerland. The Soviet block nations hold an annual Tour of Berlin, Prague and Warsaw.

I had the good fortune to be visiting Nice in southern France in the summer of 1937 and to see a stage in "The Tour." Thousands of people lined the streets to watch the champions ride into town. The champions looked very tired. Most French towns ask to be a stopover on the tour itinerary.

In 1964 on a cycling tour of France I and my tandem-pushing wife visited Paris just to see the tour finish. We purchased seats for the Parc des Princes velodrome. Every seat was taken. Before the race started motorcyclists put on a special performance of trick riding. I had looked forward to seeing a sprint finish but the riders came in singly and took a turn around the velodrome with thunderous applause. Most cheers went to Raymond Poulidor, who was defeated by his teammate Anquetil by a few seconds.

The Tour is the "World Series" of France.

The Story of Jacques Anquetil of France

This greatest of modern French racing cyclists was born January 8th, 1934. The story of his life lies in his great cycling victories:

1953	Paris-Normandie
	Grand Prix des Nations
1954	Grand Prix des Nations
1955	Champion of France
1956	Champion of France
	World Paced Record, Milan-Vel-Vigorelli
1957	Paris-Nice
	Tour de France
	Six-Day Race in Paris with Darrigade and Terruzi
1958	Grand Prix des Nations
	Six-Day Race in Paris with Darrigade and Teruzzi
1959	Grand Prix Lugano
1960	Tour de Italie
1961	Tour de France
	Paris-Nice
1962	Tour de France
1963	Tour de France
	Paris-Nice
	Vuelta de Espagne
1964	Tour de France
	Tour de Italie
1965	Paris-Nice
	Grand Prix des Nations

FAUSTO COPPI LEADING THE TOUR
Courtesy of United Press International

EDDY MERCKX OF BELGIUM
Photo by Robert F. George
Velo-News

When Anquetil was four years old his father Ernest bought him a bicycle. He learned to balance it in less than an hour. He soon made up his mind to be a bicycle racer. He studied the racing styles of Bobet, Coppi, Bartali, Magne, Van Steenbergen, and others.

The Story of Fausto Coppi of Italy

Coppi was born in Italy in 1917. At an early age he decided to become a racing cyclist. An uncle who saw him win a race predicted, "Some day you will be a great bicycle racer." He trained hard and long and reached world championship class. The Italian champion Gino Bartali, whom he planned to defeat some day, was his idol. The day came in the 1950's in a match race.

He won several important victories in international competition:

World Road Championship in 1953
World Professional Pursuit Champion in 1947
Tour de France winner in 1949 and 1952
Five times winner of the Tour of Italy
Five times winner of the Tour of Lombardy
Set the one hour unpaced record of 28 miles 805 yards at the Milan Velodrome Vigorelli
Twice Winner Grand Prix des Nations

At the height of his career 1953-55 he was reputed to be the highest paid professional athlete in the world. Willy Kutschbach, a German racer, author of *Fausto Coppi*, rates him the greatest racing professional of all time.

Fausto Coppi died on January 2, 1960 of bronchial pneumonia. During his twenty active years he had made a phenomenal career as a professional cyclist. Italy considers him as one of her immortal sons.

The Story of Eddy Merckx of Belgium

This young Belgian cyclist is rated in the superior class of riders along with Anquetil, Coppi and Harris. He was born in Meensel Kiezegem, Belgium on June 17, 1945.

His story is in his phenomenal winnings:

Tour de France winner 1969, 1970, 1971, 1972, and 1974 (This is considered the greatest bicycle race in the world.)
Winner Milan - San Remo
  " Tour de Romandie
  " Tour of Sardinia
  " Tour of Belgium
  " Tour de Flanders
  " Paris-Roubaix
  " Liege- Bastogne- Liege
  " Giro Italie
World Speed Record - Paced Olympic Veledrome in Mexico, 1972.

Six-Day Races:
  Antwerp 1974, 1975, 1976 with partner Patrick Sercu
  Gent 1975 with Patrick Sercu
  Grenoble 1973 and 1975 with Patrick Sercu
  Milan 1971 with Stevens
  Rotterdam 1976 with Patrick Sercu
World Championship - The Greatest Distance covered in one hour unpaced 30 miles and 125 yards on the Velodrome Olympic, in Mexico.
  He is a national hero of Belgium and the most successful rider in the history of the sport.

Six-Day Race Winners

The Six-Day Bicycle Race Story

The Pictorial World published in London on November 30, 1878 reported as follows: "On Monday November 18, 1878 a six-day bicycle race commenced at six o'clock in the evening at Agricultural Hall for the Championship of the World. The riders were permitted to use any size of wheel and could be changed at will. The track was eight laps to the mile. Leading competitors among the twelve starters were John Keen, champion of England, C. Terrant, champion of France, D. Stanton and W. Cann of England, both long distance champions. On Saturday night W. Cann won the gold medal having ridden 1,051 miles 5 ½ laps on his Stanley bicycle."

The early six-day races were endurance contests. A rider pedalled about 12 hours out of 24, stopping for nourishment and a catnap before continuing again. In the first six-day race held in Chicago in November 1879 the contestants rode 14 hours a day.

In the first continuous six-day races held in New York in 1891 each competitor rode as long as he was able. The top international riders in these competitions were Mills of England, Terrant of France and Miller of America. Reporter Victor Breyer, an official of the International Cyclists Union, considered Charles Miller the greatest endurance champion of all time.

The first two-man team six-day race was held in Madison Square Garden in New York in 1899. This race was won by Charles Miller and Frank Waller. Since that date 68 six-day races have been held in New York's Madison Square Garden. These popular races have been conducted in 84 cities around the world. They are still popular and are held yearly in Berlin, Brussels, Cologne, Copenhagen, Dortmund, Frankfurt, Ghent, Milan, Montreal, Zurich, and elsewhere.

SIX-DAY BICYCLE RACE By Joseph DeMartini
Courtesy of the St. Louis Art Museum, Eliza McMillan Fund

During World War II, when foreign riders were unable to come to America to compete, interest waned. Ice hockey and basketball became more popular.

Six-Day Champions

Here is a sketch of the lives and records of a few world famous six-day champions:

Alfred Goullet is unquestionably one of the greatest six day riders in the world. He was born in Australia in 1891; he came to America at an early age and acquired United States citizenship. His first victory was in the 1913 "Six", in the Garden with Joe Fogler as partner. He still holds the race record with 2,759 miles and two laps made in 1914 with Alfred Grenda. Although he won 8

six-day races in the Garden and several in the Chicago grind, he kept on riding until middle age. In 1923 he won his last six-day race. I have been a Goullet fan since 1917 when I saw my first Six–Day Race. At the Pro-Am bicycle races at Atlantic City in September of 1977 Goullet was a spectator. At 85, he still looked fit enough to compete in the 77-miler.

Goullet served in World War II at the Naval Air Station at Cape May, New Jersey. Commander Dodd reports that Goullet was as fine a machine gun instructor as he was a bike rider. "Alf" was a gentleman on or off the track. In 1961 he was elected to the American Bicycle Hall of Fame.

51

Below:
ALFRED GOULLET, OUR CHAMPION 1914

Courtesy of Alfred Goullet

To Roland Geist with kind regards from Alf Goullet

Alfred Letourneur - Alfred was born in Amiens, France, July 25, 1907. He was one of the most popular all-around champions to compete in the United States.

Six times Letourneur won six-day races in New York teamed with French, Belgian and Italian riders, including the great Franco Giorgetti. He won the American motor paced championship three times in a row. In 1938 and 1941 he held the world's paced speed record at over 108 miles an hour. When he was 68 years of age he competed in the Pepsi Cola 24-hour marathon in Central Park.

Alfred passed away in 1975. Madame Letourneur is still very active in the cycling sport. During the past few years she has been the official starter of the annual Kennedy Memorial Bicycle Race held in Central Park under the auspices of the Century Road Club Association. At the 1977 race the Cadet Cycling Team came down from West Point and won several prizes, with their women cadets in the cheering section.

I had the pleasure of cycling with the champion early Sunday mornings in Central Park, accompanied by Ben Mirto of the Union Sportiva Italiano.

Franco Giorgetti - This great Italian champion was born in Italy in 1899. In 1926 he won his first six-day bike race at New York's Madison Square Garden, teamed with Reggie MacNamara. He was one of the smallest competitors to race on the track, but he won six Garden races. Franco had a big cheering section whenever he competed in the six-day events. A reporter writes, "When he decides to win a sprint, he will pedal out from the rear, like a shot out of a gun, to outride his opponents."

Reginald J. MacNamara - He was born in Australia on November 7, 1888. He came to America in 1913 and,

52

although becoming a U.S. citizen, still competed for his native land in the races. He won five six-day events, teamed with the popular Giorgetti and Linari of Italy. Reggie was known as the "Iron Man of Cycling." One time, while training on his bicycle, he suffered a fractured skull, but in a few weeks he was out riding again. He was still competing in these races when he was well past the age of fifty - a remarkable record.

Kilian and Vopel - This German six-day team was billed as "The Cycling Sensations of Madison Square Garden." As a team they won four New York races.

Gustav Killian - He was born in Luxembourg, Germany, November 3, 1907. He started his cycling career as an amateur. He won twenty races in Germany and America.

Heinz Vopel - Vopel was born in Dortmund, Germany, April 5, 1908. He competed in six-day races in Europe, but had his greatest success in the United States and Canada. Teamed with his partner Kilian, he won ten straight six-day events in New York, Chicago, Montreal, Milwaukee and London. A reporter writes, "They blazed a triumphant trail across America." The public tired of seeing this team win again and again, so the managers decided to break up the partners. With other teammates they were not so successful.

Peter Post - This professional road and track cyclist was born in the Netherlands in 1933. He was the national pursuit champion and European motor paced champion.

Post won the 1964 Paris Roubaix race with a record speed of over 28 miles an hour. He is best known for his 56 victories in six-day racing, beating the Van Steenberg record of 40 victories.

World's Leading Six-Day Race Winners

Number of Races	Name	Country
65	Peter Post	Holland
48	Patrick Sercu	Belgium
40	Rik Van Steenbergen	Belgium
38	Willy Peden	Canada
37	Klaus Bugdahl	Germany
34	Gustav Kilian	Germany
33	Fritz Pfenninger	Sweden
32	Piet Van Kempen	Holland
32	Heinz Vopel	Germany
25	Emile Severeyne	Belgium
25	Dieter Kemper	Germany
23	Rudi Altig	Germany
23	Fernando Terruzzi	Italy
23	Sigl Renz	Germany
21	Alfred Letourneur	France
21	Palle Lykke Jensen	Denmark
21	Rene Pijnen	Holland
19	Reg.Mac Namara	Australia
19	Gerrit Schulte	Holland
17	Gerard Debaets	Belgium
17	Jan Pijnenburg	Holland
16	Reg. Arnold	Australia
16	Leo Duyndam	Holland
16	Sid Patterson	Australia
16	Jean Roth	Sweden
16	Cecil Yates	USA
15	Alfred Goullet	Australia

OLYMPIA—THE ANCIENT STADIUM, 776 B.C.
Courtesy of the Greek National Tourist Office, New York City

The Olympic Games

Olympia

"To set the cause above renown,
To love the game beyond the prize
To honor as you strike him down
The foe that comes with fearless eyes,
To count the life of battle good,
And dear the land that gave you birth
And dearer yet the Brotherhood,
That binds the brave of all the Earth."

Author Unknown

The Olympic Cyclists Oath

"We swear that we will take part in the Olympic Games in loyal competition, respecting the regulations which govern them and desirous of participating in them in the true spirit of sportsmanship for the honor of our country and the glory of the sport."

The Olympic Motto
Citius - Altius - Fortius
Swifter - Higher - Stronger

Bicycling in the Olympic Summer Games

The ancient Olympic Games were first celebrated in 776 B.C. at Olympia in Greece, where the first stadium still stands. These games were held during the summer every

OLYMPIA—THE MODERN STADIUM, ATHENS 1896
Courtesy of the Greek National Tourist Office, New York City

four years to honor Zeus. They were the most important and popular festival of the ancient Greek world.

The modern revival of the Olympic Games is due largely to the efforts of Baron Pierre de Coubertin (1863-1937) of France. In 1894 he initiated a conference in Paris which resulted in the 1896 Olympics held in Athens, in a white marble stadium near the center of the city. After his death, Coubertin was honored by having his heart enshrined in a sacred monument near the ancient stadium.

Great Olympic Champions

Marcus Hurley of the United States won the most gold Olympic cycling medals in the history of the Games. At St. Louis in 1904 he won the 1/4, 1/3, 1/2 and mile championships.

Track cyclists who won three gold medals were: Paul Masson of France, Francisco Verri of Italy and Robert Charpentier of France.

Daniel Morelon of France won seven gold Olympic medals during the period 1966 to 1973. He is considered one of the greatest amateur champions of all time.

In 1912 C. Shutte of the United States won a bronze medal in Olympic track cycling.

Jack Simes - U.S.A.

Jack is our best-known and most admired modern American track racing cyclist. He was born in Teaneck, New Jersey on November 20, 1942. Both father and grandfather were racing champions.

A brief outline of his great competitive accomplishments starts with the winning of a Junior National

55

Championship in 1959, followed by memberships on two Pan American and three Olympic teams. In 1968 he won a second place in the World Championships at Montevideo.

In 1970 he turned professional. Among his great wins were the 1970 Odense, Denmark Grand Prix, the 1971 Aahus, Denmark Grand Prix, and a third place in the Rome Grand Prix. Jack also won the U.S.A. professional sprint championships in 1973 and 1974. He coached the U.S.A. Pan American 1975 and Olympic Track teams in 1976, and the world teams in recent years.

At present he is the Director of the Trexlertown Velodrome in Pennsylvania, Technical Director of Omni-Sports Inc., and is on the Board of Directors of Rodale Resources Inc.

In 1976 he wrote *Winning Bicycle Racing* with Barbara George, editor and publisher of *Velo-News*. The 195-page paperbound book was published by the Henry Regnery Company of Chicago. It is endorsed by the United States Cycling Federation.

I met Jack Simes at the Olympic Velodrome in Mexico at the Pan American Games in 1975. Jack has also been nominated to the American Bicycle Hall of Fame.

The Author's Participation in Olympic Cycling

1920   Tried out for the 108 mile road race held on the highways of Long Island. It was won by John Freeman of the St. Louis Cycling Club in about four and a half hours.

1932   Attended the track events at the Los Angeles Olympic Velodrome. The events were held in the cool evenings and were well attended.

1971   On a cycling tour of Greece visited the site of the ancient Olympic stadium. Rode to the site of the shrine dedicated to Baron Pierre de Coubertin. The guide was one of the Greek runners who carried the Olympic Flame.

1972   Member of the XX Olympic Cycling Trials Committee Awarded The Certificate of Participation

1972   Attended the Olympic Road Race competitions in Munich, Germany.

1975   Attended the Pan American Olympic Races in the Mexico City Velodrome. Merckx set a new world speed record on this track.

Olympic Games of the Modern Era

Olympiad Site	Date
I. Athens, Greece	1896
II. Paris, France	1900
III. St. Louis, United States	1904
IV. London, England	1908
V. Stockholm, Sweden	1912
VI. Berlin, Germany (Not celebrated W.W. I)	
VII. Antwerp, Belgium	1920
VIII. Paris, France	1924
IX. Amsterdam, Netherlands	1928
X. Los Angeles, United States	1932
XI. Berlin, Germany	1936
XII. Tokyo and Helsinki (Not Celebrated W.W. II)	
XIII. London, England (Not Celebrated W.W. II)	
XIV. London, England	1948
XV. Helsinki, Finland	1952
XVI. Melbourne, Australia	1956
XVII. Rome, Italy	1960
XVIII. Tokyo, Japan	1964
XIX. Mexico City, Mexico	1968
XX. Munich, Germany	1972
XXI. Montreal, Canada	1976
XXII. Moscow, Soviet Union	1980
XXIII. Los Angeles, United States (?)	1984

Pan American Games

Introduction

These athletic games were organized to promote good will among the nations of the Western Hemisphere. They were conceived in 1940 by the Pan American Congress assembled in Buenos Aires, Argentina to honor the 450th anniversary of the discovery of America.

Like the Olympic Games they are held every four years, but the Pan American games are staged a year before the Olympiads.

At the 1971 Games John Howard of the U.S. won the gold medal in the 122 mile road race, at the average speed of 25.85 miles an hour. John has won many American championships on the road. A modest champion, he was elected to the American Bicycle Hall of Fame in 1973. He is presently in training to win a medal in Moscow in 1980.

At the 1975 Games in Mexico City the United States pursuit team of Paul Deem, Roger Young, Ralph Therrio and Ron S. Skarin won gold medals.

My Story

by John Howard - Our Pan American Bicycle Road Champion and Gold Medalist

I was born in Springfield, Missouri and have lived there for twenty-five years. Bicycle racing has been my life for the past six years from 1968 to date.

Most of my serious training has been done in Missouri. Geographically it was perfect for race training, located near the foothills of the Ozark Mountains. I had no less than 50 different rides, many through the scenic Mark Twain National Forest, which is nice any time of the year. During the early months of the year, I would average 300-400 miles per week, most of which was joy riding through the forest.

The United States Army stabilized life for me in 1970. I was only a few hours short of a B.F.A. degree when they drafted me out of Southwest Missouri State University. I had used up my student deferment, having lost a semester in 1968 while competing on the Olympic team. During my army career cycling became serious - it was either that or Viet Nam. I won one of my three national championships and a gold medal at California in the Pan American Games while serving, and I appreciate that support. I doubt if I will ever be quite so dedicated to anything again.

Sincerely,
January 22nd 1973   *John Howard*

Pan American Games of the Modern Era

Number	Site		Date
I	Buenos Aires	Argentina	1951
II	Mexico City	Mexico	1955
III	Chicago	United States	1959
IV	San Paulo	Brazil	1963
V	Winnipeg	Canada	1967
VI	Cali	Colombia	1971
VII	Mexico City	Mexico	1975
VIII	San Juan	Puerto Rico	1979

Note: I attended the cycling events in Mexico City in 1975

Racing Bibliography

Anquetil, Jacques, *Je Suis Comme Ca,* Union General, Paris, 1964.

Baranet, Nancy N., *The Turned Down Bar,* Dorrance, Philadelphia, 1964.

Bobet, Louison and LeBert, R., *En Selle,* Edition Points, Paris, 1958.

Bowden, Kenneth, *Cycle Racing,* Temple Press, London, 1958.

Briquet, Georges, *60 Ans de Tour de France,* La Table Ronde, Paris, 1962.

Brunwin, Douglas, *Annals of a Racing Cyclist,* Private, Herts, 1944.

Chassignon, Andre, *La Tour de France,* Le Grande Corse, Paris, 1952.

Clifford, Peter, *The Tour de France,* Stanley Paul, London, 1965.

Daily Express, *The First Tour of Britain,* Daily Express, London, 1961.

Fearnley, Charles, *The Story of the Six,* Sporting Record, London, 1949.

Grandmaison, Mario, *Le Tour de France,* Librarie Lafevre, Paris, 1960.

Harris, Reg., *Biography by George Pearson,* Temple Press, London, 1950.

Jauneu, Marc, *Le Cyclisme de Coppi, Van Looy, etc.,* Darguad, Paris, 1967.

Kutschbach, Willy, *Fausto Coppi,* Kutschbach, Berlin, 1954.

Michard, Lucien-Revaud, Andre *Le Cyclisme sur Piste,* Borneman, Paris

Mills, Bill, *Olympic Cycling,* Oliver Moxon, London, 1948.

Mironer, Pavel D., *Bicycle Racing,* 1958.

Mockridge, Russell, *My World on Wheels,* Stanley Paul, London, 1960.

Pelissier, Henri, *Le Cyclisme sur Route,* Borneman, Paris, 1950.

Pearson, George, *Reg Harris,* Temple Press, London, 1950.

Poulidor Raymond, *La Gloire sans Maillot Jaune,* Calman, Paris, 1968.

Ruys, Charles, *Spotlight 6 Day Races,* Bernicotts Ltd., London, 1967.

St. Pierre, Roger, *Louison Bobet,* Kennedy Bros., Yorkshire, 1972.

St. Pierre, Roger, *The Story of Reg Harris,* Kennedy Bros., Yorkshire, 1972.

Simes, Jack, *Winning Bicycle Racing,* Henry Regnery Co., Chicago, 1976.

Simpson, Tommy, *Cycling is My Life,* Stanley Paul, London, 1966.

Swan, Dick, *The Life and Times of Charley Barden,* Wunlap Publications, Leicester, 1965.

Swan, Dick, *Bert Harris of the Polly,* System Printing, Leicester, 1964.

Swan, Dick, *Days of Davies,* System Printing, Leicester, 1966.

Taylor, Marshall "Major", *The Fastest Bicycle Rider in the World,* Wormley Publishing Co., Worcester, 1928.

Taylor, Harold S., *Yorkshire's Road Racing Cyclists,* E.J. Arnold and Sons Ltd., Leeds.

Terbeen, Frances, *Les Geants du Cyclisme,* Del Duca, Paris, 1963.

Vanderstuyft, Leon and Favaud, Andre *Le Cyclisme Sur Piste Demi Fond,* Bornemann, Paris, c. 1950.

Wiley, Jack, *The Unicycle Book,* Stackpole Books, Harrisburg, Pennsylvania, 1973.

Zimmerman, A.A. and Erwin J.M., *Zimmerman Abroad and Points on Training,* Blakely, Chicago, 1895.

Racing Records

Guinness Book of World Records, Guinness, Superlatives Ltd., Enfield, England.

Velo (Annual) *Les Sports,* Rene Jacobs, Brussels, Belgium.

JOHN HOWARD, U.S.A·, WINNING THE 122-MILE ROAD RACE, PAN AMERICAN GAMES 1971
Courtesy United Press International

THE NEW LOOK AND THE OLD
Drawn by Erhart

60

4

THE WHEELWOMEN

IN THE POPULAR BROADWAY MUSICAL
"Annie Get Your Gun," Ethel Merman sings to Frank
Butler, "Any thing you can do I can do better."

Will the phenomenal performances of our racing
queens in world competition prove the truth of this song?

The Ladies Bicycle Derby

In January of 1950 two promoters organized a series of
bicycle races for 14 female competitors, mostly to come
from France, Italy, Belgium and England. A track was
built at an armory at 62nd Street and Columbus Avenue
in New York.

MARGARET GAST, CHAMPION CYCLIST AND WORLD RECORD HOLDER
Courtesy of Margaret Gast

The contract called for racing seven nights a week, four hours a night, with a salary of $25.00 a day, and a winner's prize of $1,500.00. However, American women were not interested in competing with the Europeans and the event ended as a failure. Spectators attended one night and were not thrilled. The promotors were unable to pay the European women, who ended their stay in America stranded and broke. Most of them sold their bicycles to obtain passage home.

The Queens of Speed
United States
Nancy Nieman Baranet
Connie Carpenter
Margaret Gast
Audrey McElmury
Sue Novara
Mary Jane Reoch
Sheila Young
European
Y. Reynders, *Belgium*
Beryl Burton, *Great Britain*
Eileen Sheridan, *Great Britain*
G. Ermolaeva, *Soviet Union*
T. Garkushin, *Soviet Union*
V. Savina, *Soviet Union*

Sheila Young
This world-famous bicyclist was selected in 1976 as the sportswoman of the year by Tass News Agency. Her string of victories in both cycling and speed skating are more impressive than those of the great Mildred Didrikson, Wilma Rudolph, Helen Moody and Deborah Meyer.

Sheila, a native of Detroit, Michigan, comes from a family of cycling champions, including her father, Roger Young, who was a member of the United States of America Pan American and Olympic teams, and her brother. At 26, she has twice been world champion in two sports.

A sport reporter describes this star performer as "A gracious, thoughtful, effervescent and delightful young lady who has established high standards of athletic performance to merit her choice as our Sportswoman of the Year."

(I have traveled hundreds of miles to see her compete in track races in Montreal and Atlantic City. It was thrilling to see her come from behind and win the sprint at the finish!)

In August of 1976 she married a fellow champion, Jim Ochowicz, and now has one child.

Sheila Young has been nominated unanimously for a place of honor in the American Bicycle Hall of Fame.

BERYL BURTON OF GREAT BRITIAN
Photo by Robert F. George
Velo-News

Connie Carpenter

Connie hails from Madison, Wisconsin. Starting her athletic career as a speed skater, she soon took up cycling, a related sport activity. This twenty year old woman made a great start by placing 13th in the World Road Championships in Italy.

In 1976 Connie won the United States road and pursuit championships at Louisville, thereby showing great promise as one of America's great bicycle racers.

Margaret Gast

"Aunt Margaret", as she liked to be called, was the grand lady of cycling in the Gay Nineties.

Born in Germany in 1876, she came to New York in 1890 and worked as a nurse. Miss Gast bought a bicycle in 1893, joined the Century Road Club of America, and began riding centuries with the boys. By 1896 she had won a string of century medals, and by 1900 had set many national and world records. These include:

500 Miles in 44 Hours and 45 Minutes
1000 Miles in 99 Hours and 55 Minutes
2000 Miles in 222 Hours and 5 ½ Minutes
2600 Miles in 295 Hours and 55 Minutes.

In 1906 a French woman sprint champion challenged Margaret to a race in the New York Madison Square Garden, with Margaret winning amid the acclaim of thousands of fans. The overjoyed mob came on to the track and took her bicycle apart for souvenirs of the victory. Margaret turned to motorcycle racing soon after and was called "The Mile-a-Minute Girl."

In the 1930's, she retired to a home at Pawling, New York. (I spent many afternoons with her and enjoyed hearing her life story.) The Century Road Club of America tendered her a grand testimonial banquet, and she was elected to the American Bicycle Hall of Fame.

This great lady passed on in 1968.

Audrey Mc Elmury

This world road champion was born in 1943 in Northampton, Massachusetts. At an early age she moved to San Diego, California where she attended the State College and earned a B.S. degree. She worked as a laboratory technician.

She became interested in bicycling and joined the San Diego Bicycle Club. In 1961 she led an American Youth Hostel cycling tour of Europe, but soon her interests turned to cycle racing. In 1964 she won the Southern California Women's Bicycle Championship. She kept on breaking records and winning titles, and even though she had stiff opposition from the Soviet Union racing team, she won the 1969 World's Road Racing Championship.

63

On her return she was invited to perform on a TV program, The Gary Moore Show: "To Tell The Truth." With over a million viewers watching, Gary rode her racing bicycle onto the stage and almost fell off.

Audrey is an athletic, very American woman, friendly and unassuming. She has just co-authored a new book with Mike Levonas titled *Basic Training,* published by Velo-News of Brattleboro, Vermont.

Sue Novara

One of the U.S.A.'s world bicycling champions, she hails from Flint, Michigan. Sue has represented the Wolverine-Schwinn Club with Sheila Young in racing competition. In both 1975 and 1976 she won the world sprint championships. In 1975 Sue won second place to the Soviet champion at Montreal. In national competition in 1976 she placed second in the sprints to Sheila Young. To date she has won every sprint race she competed in at the new Trexlertown Velodrome in Pennsylvania. In 1977 she won a silver medal in the World's Championships in Venezuela, in spite of the keen competition from the Soviet riders.

Mary Jane Reoch

This young Philadelphia rider began her racing career by winning the National Women's Amateur Road Race in 1971. In 1975, she went on to win the 25 Mile at the International Pro-Am Race at Atlantic City, New Jersey. Reoch also won places in world competition in 1975 at Rocourt, (a silver medal) and in 1976, at Monteroni (a bronze medal). In 1976 she was second to Connie Carpenter in the U.S.A. Road Race and second in the Pursuit Race. Her training consists of riding 40 miles in two hours each morning. If women are included in the cycling events at the 1980 Olympics, Mary will be a strong contender.

Beryl Burton of Great Britain

Beryl Burton is Britain's outstanding woman racing cyclist. Born in 1937, she began her remarkable winning career at 22. She was the British Best All-Rounder every year from 1959 to 1973. In 1967, Beryl covered 277 ¼ miles in a twelve-hour time trial and in 1968 rode 100 miles in 3 hours, 55 minutes, and 5 seconds. At Milan, in 1960, she set a world record 28 minutes 58.4 seconds for 12.4 miles. She was also the world's pursuit champion five times. For her unique performances she was awarded the "Diploma D'Honneur" by the Union Cycliste Internationale. By 1970 Beryl had won five gold medals, three silver medals and three bronze medals. Coached by the

AUDREY McELMURY, WORLD ROAD CHAMPION 1969
She is wearing the World Championship Jersey and riding the Johnny Berry bicycle used in the event.
Photo by Dan Tichonchuk

British world champion Reg Harris, she deservingly rates the title "World Cycling Queen of Speed."

Yvonne Reynders of Belgium

This greatest of Belgian women racing cyclists on both road and track was born in 1937. Yvonne won twelve world championships between 1959 and 1966. In the women's pursuit races, she won three gold and three silver medals. While on the road she took four gold and two silver prizes.

Galina Ermolaeva of The Soviet Union

One of the greatest racing champions in the Soviet Union, Galina was born in 1937, the same year as Beryl Burton, the British world champion. During her racing career, she won 14 world sprint championships and was awarded six gold, five silver and three bronze medals between 1958 and 1970.

Eileen Sheridan of Great Britian

Eileen was born in Coventry, England, the greatest bicycle manufacturing city and the home of the Bartleet Bicycle Collection. Like most people she started her cycling career with a heavy-weight touring machine, but she soon obtained a light-weight and joined the Coventry Cycling Club, a fast riding group. From time trialing she went on to racing. For her many victories she won the Bidlake Memorial Plaque. Eileen's greatest achievement was the triumphal "Land's End to John O'Groats" in two days and 11 hours, but this great event was saddened by the death of her father, her guide through her early cycling years.

The Show Girls

Before 1900
Zuila the Female Blondin

Modern
The Theron Dollies
Lilly Yokoi
Shenyang Acrobatic Troupe
  of the People's Republic of China,
  Bicycle Stabilization Feats

Zuila, The Female Blondin

Adam Forepaugh, the American show promoter, published his Annual for 1881 with an illustration of Ella Zuila, one of his top performers. "This daring, youthful little French woman," said the Annual, "accomplished the wonderful and never before attempted feat of riding a heavy velocipede backward and forward on a high wire, 100 feet in mid air above an audience of 10,000 people. During this perilous performance she maintained a relaxed and graceful position with all the poise and skill of the most accomplished bicyclist." The London Telegraph reported, "The performance given by Ella Zuila, the heroine of the high wire at the Crystal Palace, ought to satisfy the public's appetite for sensational exhibitions." The American Louisville Commercial wrote, "Ella Zuila has startled the entire city with her thrilling feat of actually riding a velocipede, backward and forward on the high wire."

Was she "The World's Last and Greatest Wonder?"

The Theron Dollies

These two queens of the tall unicycle and tiny bicycle stole the hearts of the New York Radio City Music Hall audiences a decade ago.

The unique act was billed as "Beauty on Wheels."

Lilly Yokoi

Lilly, Japanese by origin, toured the theatrical world on her bicycle. Americans have been intrigued not only by her riding, but also by her looks, costuming and stage presence. (I saw her fast-moving unique act at the New York Radio City Music Hall in December of 1961. She was billed as "The Ballerina of the Golden Bicycle.") Millions of people throughout the world had the pleasure of seeing her ride again on the evening of Sunday, May 21, 1978 when she performed on television in a show entitled, "Royal Command Circus" before the king and queen of Sweden. Lilly gave a dazzling performance as usual. After the show, she related how her father taught her cycling skills. She has been performing for over 20 years. Her home is North Bergen, New Jersey.

Shenyang Acrobatic Troupe Of The People's Republic of China, Bicycle Stablization Feats

In January of 1973, the City Center Theater in New York, the Center of Music and Drama Inc., presented the Shenyang Acrobatic Troupe of the People's Republic of China, in association with the National Committee on United States-China Relations Inc. The repertory comprised 16 acts, two of which presented the outstanding girl bicycle acrobats. Act number 5 was the "Bicycle Stabilization Feats on a Raised Platform." The three stunters needed versatile skills to balance a bicycle on a two meter high stand with steadiness and agility. Act number 8 was billed "Trick Cycling"; the three girls rode in various formations with two perched on top of the rider. Theater Reporter Clive Barnes commented on the show, "Shenyang Acrobats dazzle City Center audiences." (I enjoyed this performance thoroughly and felt it might be a step toward world peace.)

The Authors

Women Authors and Their Books On Bicycling

In the 1890's women started cycling actively. They made tremendous progress in touring, racing and recreational riding. They also wrote books about their unusual experiences.

Books published before 1900 deal mainly with learning and with bicycle care. During the last few decades general information on bicycles, touring and racing has increased greatly.

Although this chapter deals only with books by women, mention must be made of a famous American artist couple who toured Europe on both bicycles and a tandem. Joseph Pennell and Elizabeth Robins Pennell wrote jointly of their adventures awheel in Europe in the 1890's. Their books include:

A Canterbury Pilgrimage, published by Seeley and Company of London in 1885;

Our Sentimental Journey Through France and Italy, published by T. Fisher Unwin of London in 1893;

Two Pilgrim's Progress (From Fair Florence to the Eternal City of Rome), published by Little Brown and Company of Boston in 1899.

Another American cycling couple, Fanny Bullock Workman and husband, William Hunter, wrote *Algerian Memories or A Bicycle Tour Over the Atlas to the Sahara,* published by A. Randolph and Company of New York, 1890, a pioneer adventure tour.

The 22 books by women writers may be classified as: <u>Adventure</u> <u>Touring</u> - 10, <u>General</u> <u>Information</u> - 7, <u>Autobiography</u> - 1, <u>Artistic</u> <u>Cycling</u> - 1, <u>Fitness</u> - 1, <u>Novel</u> - 1, and <u>Racing</u> - 1.

Two outlines of books from American authors and two from European authors follow.

Nancy Neiman Baranet
Bicycling

This outstanding American racing bicyclist was born on January 1, 1933 in Detroit, Michigan. She attended

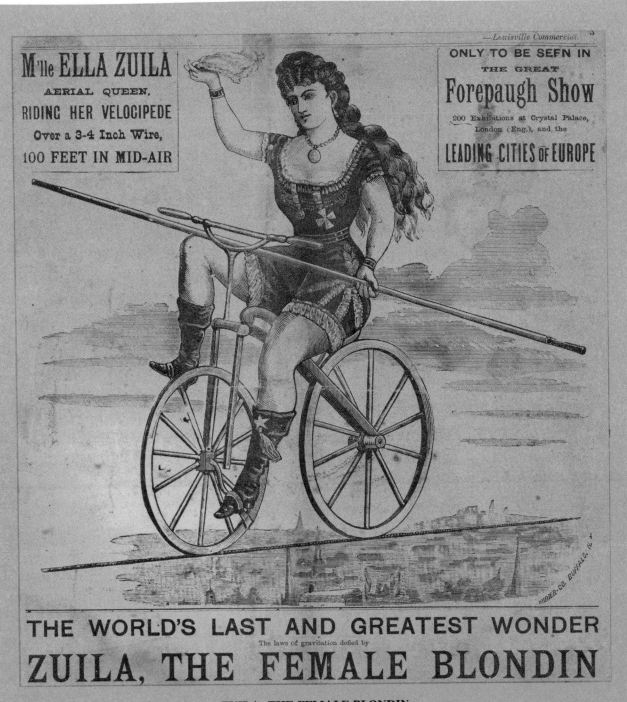

ZUILA, THE FEMALE BLONDIN
"Ella Zuila has startled the entire city with her thrilling feat of actually riding a velocipede backward and forward on the high wire."
Courtesy of Adam Forepaugh Circus Annual 1881

Yokoi

Detroit Business University. She started her cycling career as a member of the American Youth Hostels but soon turned to racing. Nancy won the National Championships in 1953, 1954, 1956 and 1957, and tied the existing World Record in 1956 at 200 meters. She married her trainer in 1957 and is the mother of five children. Nancy has been a Director of the Amateur Bicycle League of America since 1956. Currently she is the editor of the "Racing" page of *The American Bicyclist and Motorcyclist,* the oldest bicycle trade journal in the country.

With such a complete cycling background, she has written a most informative book entitled *Bicycling,* published by A. S. Barnes and Company, and also a racing book entitled *The Turned Down Bar. Bicycling* contains over 200 pictures and diagrams of great interest to every rider. It contains information on buying a bicycle, touring, maintenance, and cycle camping.

Eileen Sheridan
Wonder Wheels

One of the most outstanding women long distance cyclists in Great Britain, Eileen Sheridan began cycling on a typical heavyweight machine at age 14. She joined the Coventry Cycling Club and started riding mileage. Her enthusiasm, stamina and determination helped her break long distance records.

Though she was a housewife and mother, Eileen spent much of her time training. Her greatest feat was her triumphant "End to End" ride from Land's End to John O'Groats in two days and 11 hours, a distance of 872 miles through the roads of England and Scotland. She made a second record by riding 1000 miles in three days and one hour. Eileen was managed by the British men's record holder Frank Southall. She also held the title of "British Best All-Rounder" for two years in succession, and rode 237 5/6 miles in 12 hours. Mr. Southall writes, "In spite of all the headlines Eileen still remains completely unspoiled and is always ready to give advice and help to any young enthusiast who asks for advice."

In her fascinating book *Wonder Wheels* she has most interesting chapters! These include "How It All Started," "The Fun of Club Life," "Success in My First Year," and "Twelve at Last."

Maria E. Ward
Bicycling For Ladies

Back in 1896, when this book was written, Miss Ward opened the preface with "I have found that in bicycling, as in other sports enjoyed by women and girls, they bring upon themselves censure from many sources." Those were the days when women were expected to stay home and take care of the family. However, women in the public eye, like the actress Lillian Russell and newspaper editor Ella Wheeler Wilcox, showed that a lady could be dignified and still pedal a bicycle in Central Park.

The newly organized Michaux Cycling Club, comprised of many of the New York elite (the "Four Hundred") rode both outdoors and indoors during the Gay Nineties. A club rule barred all bloomer-clad riders. The men wore the usual knicker suits and caps.

Bicycling for Ladies, published by Brentanos in 1896, contained 200 pages with 34 illustrations, probably posed by Miss Ward herself. She offers practical information with chapters: "For Beginners," "The Art of Wheeling," "Position and Power," "Tools and How to Use Them," "Tires," "Adjustments," "Dress," "Mechanics of the Bicycle," and "Exercise and Training."

She ended her book with, "Take the bicycle as it is, use it intelligently, enjoy it, and become an enthusiast."

Dervla Murphy
Full Tilt

The author of this most unusual bicycle touring adventure was born in County Waterford, Ireland on November 28, 1931. Her father was the County Librarian. Dervla was educated at the Ursuline Convent in Waterford. She continued her education by reading travel and adventure books. In 1963 she made a bold decision to pedal a bicycle alone from her Ireland home to India.

She realized the dangers of touring alone to countries where women, especially traveling alone, are not treated with respect, so she carried a pistol to be used only in dire emergency. The tour through desert and jungle entailed punctures, broken ribs, hornets and scorpions. Her Islamic hosts en route, however, provided her with necessary services.

Her route from Ireland took her through England, France, Yugoslavia, Bulgaria, Turkey, Iran, Afghanistan, Pakistan and Nepal to Delhi in India. After her daring

THE THERON DOLLIES
"Beauty on Wheels"
Courtesy of the New York Radio City Music Hall

ride, she, returned to her home in Waterford. She had liked the people of Nepal and decided to go back to India, this time via plane. She settled in Nepal for seven months and found work in a Tibetan refugee camp. Dervla described her months in India in a book entitled, *The Waiting Land—A Spell in Nepal,* published by John Murray of London in 1967.

A critic said of the author, "Dervla is a brave, intelligent, a rare and amusing human being."

Books on Bicycling Written By Women

Baranet, Nancy Neiman, *The Turned Down Bar,* Dorrance, Philadelphia, 1964.

Baranet, Nancy Neiman, *Bicycling,* A. S. Barnes and Co., New Jersey, 1973.

Davidson, Lillian Campbell, *Handbook for Lady Cyclers,* Hay Nisbet and Co., London, 1896.

Duncan, Shirley, *Two Wheels to Adventure,* George C. Herrap Co., London, 1957.

Erskine, Miss F. J., *Lady Cycling,* Walter Scott Ltd., London c., 1896.

Fox, Dorothea M., *Pedalling to Adventure,* Torch-Cedar Rapids, 1940.

Healey, Dorothy, *All About Bicycles,* Comet Press, New York, 1957.

Kennard, Mrs. Edward, *A Guide Book for Lady Cyclists,* F. V. White, London, 1896.

Kennard, Mrs. Edward, *The Golf Lunatic and His Cycling Wife,* Brentanos, New York, 1902.

Marks, Isabel, *Fancy Cycling,* Sands and Co., London, 1901.

McCray, Florine Thayer and Smith, Esther Louise, *Wheels and Whims,* Cupples Upham Co., Boston, 1884.

McElmury, Audrey and Mike Levonas, *Basic Training,* Velo-News, 1967.

Murphy, Dervla, *Full Tilt,* John Murray, London, 1965.

Murphy, Dervla, *A Spell in Nepal—The Waiting Land,* John Murray, London, 1967.

Nelson, Janet, *Biking for Fun and Fitness,* Award Books, New York, 1970.

Pennoll, Elizabeth Robbin, *Over the Alps on a Bicycle,* Unwin, London, 1898.

Sheridan, Eileen, *Wonder Wheels,* N. Kaye, London, 1956.

Sutherland, Louise, *I Follow the Wind,* Southern Cross, London, 1962.

Ward, Marie E., *Bicycling for Ladies,* Brentanos, New York, 1896.

Willard, Frances E., *A Wheel Within a Wheel,* Fleming Revell, New York, 1895.

Workman, Fannie B. and William, *Sketches Awheel in Modern Iberia,* G. Putnam Sons, New York, 1897.

Workman, Fannie B. and William, *Algerian Memories,* A. Randolph and Co., New York, c. 1890.

Young, Elizabeth and Jim, *Bicycle Built for Two,* Binfords and Mort, Portland, Oregon, 1940.

LADIES CYCLING COSTUME OF 1896
Courtesy of *The Ladies Tailor*

Bicycle Fashion

Amelia Jenks Bloomer and Ladies Bicycle Fashions

This pioneer designer of ladies cycling attire was born in 1818 in Cortland County, New York. She married Dexter J. Bloomer, a lawyer, whose name she immortalized.

The garment she designed was similar to trousers worn in Moslem harems. It kept a woman's legs covered decently without restricting her freedom of action. Mrs.

70

**THE BLOOMER GIRL —
MEN ADMIRE YOUR ATTIRE**
By K. L. Connor, 1895

Bloomer was active in the early women's campaign for dress reform and women's rights. In 1854 she edited and published a magazine named *The Lily,* devoted to equal rights.

Colonel Albert Pope, the Yankee bicycle manufacturer, did much to popularize the bloomer by advertising a bloomer girl astride his famous Columbia bicycle.

Mrs. Reginald de Koven, a noted stage personality of the period, wrote in *Cosmopolitan* magazine of August 1895, that "To men rich and poor, the bicycle is an unmixed blessing, but to the woman it is deliverance, revolution and salvation. Since women have taken up the bicycle it has become more and more apparent every day that its use demands a more or less radical change in their costume. Women who ride a great deal have adopted the short skirt, or the bloomers or knickerbocker costume."

In modern times, the female cyclist has many choices: slacks, pedal pushers, knickers, and short-shorts. Today, fashion designers and buyers for the big stores set the styles for cycling. On the first New Haven Railroad Cycle Train from New York to the Berkshires in 1936, R. H. Macy and Company staged a bicycle fashion show en route. Professional models presented cycling fashions of 1890 and 1936. The new styles included divided skirts, or culottes, and knickers in corduroy and gabardine. The happy but tired riders were provided with free beer on the return ride.

Bloomers

Some observing man discovered
    (How I've never thought to ask)
That Kentucky maidens' bloomers
    Have a pocket for a flask;
That the cycling girl of Texas
    As she rides is not afraid
She provides a pistol-pocket
    When she has her bloomers made;
That the bloomer-girl of Boston
    Always cool and wisely frowning,
Has a pocket in her bloomers,
    Where she carries Robert Browning;
That the Daisy Bell of Kansas,
    Who has donned the cycling breeches,
Has a pocket in her bloomers
    Full of women suffrage speeches;
That Chicago's wheeling woman,
    When her cycle makes rotations,
Has a special bloomer pocket
    Where she carries pork quotations;
That Milwaukee's cycling beauties,
    As they pedal day by day,
Have a tiny secret pocket
    Where a corkscrew's stowed away;
That the Gotham bloomer damsel,
    Whom Manhattan dudes admire,
Has a tutti-frutti pocket
    Full of gum to mend her tire.

From the Toledo, Ohio *Bee*

Lady Cycling During the Victorian Days In England

English women who rode bicycles at the turn of the century were considered freakish and decidedly unfeminine. Practically no woman rode the hobby horse, boneshaker or ordinary high-wheel. However, they rode the tricycle in the 1880's. The invention of the drop frame

A DARING GIRL OF THE GAY NINETIES

and pneumatic tire made cycling more pleasurable to women. These improvements resulted in both indoor and outdoor cycling schools and new riding fashions.

Lady Harberton organized a "Rational Dress League." All members pledged themselves to wear the new bloomer costume or knicker styles when cycling in public. The campaign shocked many people. One wheelwoman was stopped by a police officer and told to go home and put on a skirt.

Marguerite Wilson wrote in *Cycling* for 1946, "Those girls of the bloomer period must have been extremely interesting personalities and deserve our undying admiration for the performance they accomplished. They continued to persevere in spite of the adverse public opinion, and in gratitude to their lead it is up to us to carry on the great tradition they molded in those daring days."

Most of the ladies cycling clubs of the period considered racing undignified, and stated so in their rules and regulations, though some daring women did violate all conventions by racing. A Mrs. Ward, wearing a conservative long-skirted dress and hat, and riding a heavy touring bicycle equipped with mud guards, gear case and heavy tires, established a Brighton-and-back record of about six and a half hours over poor roads. Maggie Foster, paced by a motorcycle, did the Brighton-and-back in five and a half hours. Kate Green of York covered 300 miles in 24 hours, unpaced. These were astonishing performances by Victorian women.

Bicycle Poetry About Women

Poems

"Wrecked"	Anonymous
"The New Women"	Ida Trafford Bell
"Learning to Ride the Bicycle"	Grace Duffie Boylan
"Dames of Washington"	Grace Duffie Boylan
"To Alice"	Famous Lady Cyclists
"Marie's First Ride"	Marie
"Ho! For The Wheel"	Margaret E. Sangster
"King Tommy's Rise and Fall"	Ella Wheeler Wilcox

Wrecked

A girl, a wheel,
A shock, a squeal
A header, a thump,
A girl in a lump,
A bloomer all torn,
A maiden forlorn.

The New Woman.

She never grows old, no, it isn't the mode,
She has pinned her faith to the "fresh air" code,
And joined the gay throng out on the road.
Her grandma wore cute, little lacy caps,
Her grandma took daily, her little naps,
But she takes the air in modern wraps.
Her grandma grew aged at forty or so;
But stemming the tide of the long ago,
Her locks show but faintest trace of snow.
Now she, when at sixty, her countenance bright,
Her cheeks smooth and ruddy, her step soft and light,
A woman of thirty in vigor and might.
When heavy her burdens and trials may feel,
And she, for herself, some sweet solace would steal,
She instinctively turns to her tried friend, the wheel.
When once in the saddle, out 'neath the blue sky,
Like a bird on its pinions, she seemeth to fly,
Her burdens are lifted, her spirits soar high.
She dwells not on mem'ries of joys that are flown,
How fleeting they were to her has been shown--
Now, dependent on none, she goes forth alone.
This, then, is the "up to date,""New Woman's" code,
This Nineteenth Century's practical mode
Of defying the years by "the fresh air code."

Ida Trafford Bell
Imperial Magazine

Learning to Ride the Bicycle
Rhymed Rules for Women

To mount the wheel with perfect grace
First see the pedals are in place;
The right, the center half around,
The left, the nearest to the ground
Draw back the wheel a little thus,
To give it proper impetus
Your hands upon the handle bar
Should be as saintly touches are,
Then press the right foot, till you see
The inside pedal rising free
Don't be in haste, the pedal right
Describes the circle, sinks from sight;
But ere it meets your foot, once more
You've mounted and the lessons o'er.

Grace Duffie Boylan, 1896

Dames of Washington

The Capital ladies are gloomy this year,
And the pavements of Washington lonely appear
Because the good President thinks it his right
To put his foot down with 300 pound might
On bicycle riding for women of place
Lest some of their thoughts take the bicycle pace

And then the wheel costume, though modest it be,
He thinks unbecoming to dames of degree
And says with a frown quite forbidding and grim,
That Cabinet ladies must listen to him;
Their husbands he hires for wars and such like
To give him more leisure to cope with the "bike"

And while they are puzzling o'er Cuban affairs
And over wise statecraft are splittin fine hairs,
The President keeps weather eyes over the town
(Like Officer Rowan of local renown)
And when ever on a wheel a fine lady he sees
He sends her right home just as cool as you please.

The beautiful streets of the Capital gay
Are made by a prophet, the wheelwomen say
Each one is as smooth as a ribbon of white
With all its magnificant distance in sight,
And if one's abroad in the fresh morning hours,

The country breeze brings her the essence of flowers
The ladies of Washington bow to their fate
And find at a ball or dinner of state
The sole recreation propriety yields
Though they sigh at the freedom of pony-set fiends,
And say as they murmur their wishes so strong
"Well Mr. G. Cleveland, you can't boss us long."

Grace Duffie Boylan
Wheel Talk, April 23, 1896

(P.S.: Bicyclists of the 1970's have come a long way since 1896 when
Miss Boylan composed this pleading poem.)

To Alice

"The courtly dames of old Versailles sedan chairs rode,
you know;
The Russian has her droshky, and her sledge the Esqui-
maux;
The Irish lass, a jumping car; a coach for London swells;
But lovely Alice on her wheel is fleetest of the belles."

Famous Lady Cyclists
London, 1890

Marie's First Ride

How well do I recall
Those pleasant nights in fall,
When I was being taught
    To ride a wheel.
A bicycle, it's true, is best
When not in use,
But standing up beside
    A good old tree.
If that bicycle could talk
As fast as it could walk,
    'Tis hard to guess
What stories it might tell;
For I learned my lesson best
While we sat down to rest
And the bicycle leaned
    Against a good old tree.

Marie
Boston Globe

Ho! For The Wheel.

It's ho! for a ride in the open,
    With the cool winds blowing free,
And nothing but joy on dale and hill
    For my trusty wheel and me,
It's ho! for the dew of the morning
    That sparkles on leaf and spray,
And ho! for the charm of the sunset light
    When the glad day fades away.
With muscles that answer quickly
    To call of the resolute will,
With cheeks that glow and eyes that shine
    And pulses that bound and thrill,
I fly through the beautiful kingdom
    That beckons my wheel and me,
Queen of the world of girlhood,
    And sovereign of all I see.

Margaret E. Sangster

74

King Tommy's Rise and Fall.

Tommy was ruled by his father and mother,
Tommy was bossed by his older brother.
Tommy was tyrannized over each hour
By the very small maid with the face of a flower,
But one day Tommy was given a wheel
And he felt like a king on a throne of steel.
Now a sudden rise from a serf to a king
Has always proven a dangerous thing.
The people who come into power too quick
Go up like a rocket and down like a stick.
King Tom, before the first day was done,
Was Emperor, Sultan, and Czar in one.
He owned the pavement, he owned the street,
He ran the officers off their beat,
He frightened the coachmen out of their wits
As he scorched right under their horses' bits.
Pedestrians fled when they saw him approach,
He caused disaster to carriage and coach;
For he never turned out and his pace never slowed;
His bell was a signal to clear the road;
And I would not repeat, indeed, not I,
What the truckmen said when his bike went by.
King Tom only winked in their eyes with a grin,
Proud of his power to make them sin.
And bolder and bolder each day he grew,
And faster and faster his bicycle flew;
And he was certain he owned the earth
And all that was on it from girth to girth.
And he always got off without hurt or scratch,
Till all of a sudden he met his match.
Reigning one time in his usual splendor,
He came face to face with a Cable's fender.
He rang his bell for the right of way,
But a biker may ring till his hair turns gray,
And a Cable Car or its Cousin Trolley
Will pay no heed to that sort of folly.
All that King Tom recalls of that day
Was riding into the milky way,
Where he saw all the stars in the heavens.
Well, There isn't much more of his reign to tell.
He gave his wheel to his brother Bill
And walks on two crutches and always will.
And he says as he looks at his wooden leg,
"I went up like a rocket and down like a peg."

Ella Wheeler Wilcox, *The Sun*

THE WOMAN CYCLIST
By Lowenheim, 1896

75

THE UGO ANCILLOTTI TROUPE
French bicycle experts and unicycle riders
Courtesy of the New York Historical Society

5

THE SHOW PEOPLE

FOR THE PAST HUNDRED YEARS THE "GREAT-est Show on Earth" has included bicycle and unicycle acts in its productions. At the 108th Ringling Brothers Barnum and Bailey Combined Shows there were two spectacular cycling acts. The King Charles Troupe, composed of New York City youths, presented a dazzling basketball game on unicycles. From Bulgaria the Kon-dovi Troupe, on tour for the first time in America, pedaled their unicycles in pyramid formation on the high wire. It was a breath-taker.

Other cycling acts were held at the New York Radio City Music Hall, the Winter Garden, the Palace Theatre

**LES FRERES ANCILLOTTI WITH
BARNUM AND BAILEY SHOWS**
Courtesy of the New York Historical Society

The Stirk Family

The Original Trick and Fancy Bicyclists of America

The Four Great Artists

Professor T. Stirk, Mlle, Laura Stirk, Mr. Denny Stirk and the greatest child bicyclist in the world, Mlle. Flora Stirk.

Every Act New and Startling

The most elegant costumes in the country. Single, double, triple and quadruple riding on one, two, three and four machines. The Stirk family are known around the country for their daring and picturesque riding. Their names are a household word throughout America and England, having appeared before the crowned heads of Europe. They were invited to America by the Honorable P. T. Barnum and have appeared in the principal theaters here.

Popular Prices of Admission

Professor T. Stirk	Will Sibson
Proprietor	Business Manager

From a Single Poster
c. 1880

and on television. I have seen every modern act mentioned in this chapter. I consider the Great Wallandas, the Kondovi Troupe, Joe Jackson, and Steve McPeak the greatest performers.

Three outstanding films with cycling themes were Academy Award winners: "The Bicycle Thief," "The Song of the Open Road," and "Six Day Bike Rider," which featured comedian Joe E. Brown.

Readers interested in bicycle show business may visit the Library and Museum of the Performing Arts at the Lincoln Center in New York City.

Show People

Les Freres Ancillotti

A troupe of daring French bicycle acrobats who did double simultaneous loops and jumped the quadruple chasms. Described as the climax of all death-defying deeds, they performed at about the turn of the century.

Boy Foy

In April of 1947 I had the pleasure of seeing this unique unicyclist perform at Radio City Music Hall in New York. Boy Foy was kind enough to send me an autographed picture of himself performing his difficult act.

Theater critics in various cities have reviewed his act as follows:

Kansas City

"Outstanding unicyclist and juggler. His routine includes the best juggling tricks--and he does them while on the cycle. Later he works on the high unicycle."

Pittsburgh

"Boy Foy juggles while speeding about the stage, first on a low unicycle, then on a high one. Only once Foy was off form, missing a trick."

New York

"Boy Foy cuts loose with his juggling high jinks. There isn't an idle second in his act. Indian clubs, rubber balls, devil sticks and revolving disks are included in Foy's top-notch juggling performance."

The Six Frielanis

In May of 1962 the Six Frielanis performed at New York Radio City Music Hall. They were billed as "Cycling Acrobatic Stars." They presented an act with both unicycling and formation riding on bicycles.

I enjoyed the production and added to a big round of applause.

BOY FOY
Courtesy of the New York Radio City Music Hall

THE SIX FRIELANIS
Courtesy of the New York Radio City Music Hall

79

The Story of the Jacksons - Senior and Junior

Joe Jackson, whose real name was Joseph Franz Jiranek, was born in Vienna on January l, 1880. His father had a coffee house in the city. Joe Jackson, Jr. writes this story about his famous father:

"My dad was very interested in sports, especially cycling. He became noted for his trick riding and won quite a few races when he was young. At about the age of seventeen he challenged an American polo cyclist, who at the time was the world champion. Dad won and never was defeated after that. He had an old British chum as a partner, and they traveled all over Europe with their polo cycling team. While working in the Crystal Palace in London, he created his famous silent comedy, the break-away bicycle act. This act became his main entertainment and was an immediate success on stages in both America and Europe. He starred at Radio City Music Hall in New York, Moulin Rouge in Paris, Tivoli Gardens in Copenhagen, and in the Sonja Henie and Wirtz Ice Shows in America. Dad passed away on May 14, 1942 at the old Roxy Theatre in New York of a heart attack. He lived to make people laugh and did indeed leave them laughing."

Joe Jackson Jr., is now performing his father's famous act. He writes "Dad always wanted me to do the act." Although trained in engineering, he decided to follow his father's footsteps. Junior wears the same tattered tramp costume and rides the same bicycle his father rode. Recently he remarked, "Mine is a dumb act, you don't say a doggone word and there are no special tricks unless it is to keep going, without having some one fire a tomato at you." He has recently appeared in ice shows. In 1946 he married a professional ice skater, Ruth Russell.

I have had the pleasure of meeting him and receiving an autographed photograph. Junior is keeping world audiences laughing with his unique pantomine.

The Kondovi Troupe

The Kondovi Brothers began their daring high-wire cycling act in 1948. They taught their spouses, Tzetza and Stella, to perform their unique skills.

Peter is shown riding across a 30-foot high wire on a unicycle with his wife Tzetza balancing on his shoulders. The program states, "Children of all ages will hold their breath in amazement when this fearless troupe exhibit their cycling bravado in the spotlight of the Greatest Show on Earth."

I am a member of the Unicycling Society of America and have seen almost everything on one wheel, but believe this is the greatest.

Steven McPeak
The World's Highest Unicycle Rider

Dr. and Mrs. Miles S. Rogers, unicycle historians, wrote, "In 1967 Steven McPeak of Tacoma, Washington built a 32-foot-high unicycle that had an intricate gear and pedalling system. This contraption, almost four stories high, had only one disadvantage, it was so very tall that Steven had difficulty to get astride it. He solved the problem by building a taller tower from which he could mount and ride it. He would perch himself atop the unicycle at one tower, then balancing himself with his hands, set out for the opposite tower which would be as much as a hundred feet away."

This original unicycle was donated by Steven and Bill Jenack of the Unicycling Society of America, Inc. to the American Bicycle Hall of Fame Museum at Richmondtown, Staten Island, New York City, where it is on public display.

In 1978 Steven McPeak had a 101-foot-high unicycle built to his specifications. A free standing tower was also built to enable him to mount the machine.

When Steven pedals this unicycle, it will be the world's greatest aerial performance. The author has nominated him to the American Bicycle Hall of Fame.

Jack Natirboff

"Jack The Cycling Clown" does high and fancy riding on high wheel and unicycle.

He was a former racing cyclist representing the Century Road Club Association of New York in competition. Jack is an old friend and fellow club member of mine.

At the New York World's Fair of 1940 he directed the "Bicycle Ballet" number at the American Jubilee. He also has a clever bicycle comedy act which he presents at club banquets and fairs. In addition, he is usually a leader in bicycling parades in and around New York City.

He has given up racing and is the owner of "Antique Bicycle Prop Service" located at Montvale New Jersey. Here he rents antique bicycles for parades, window displays and shows.

Walter Nilsson

Nilsson was the greatest American unicycle performer. He was born during the 1890's. At seven years of age he saw a circus unicyclist and he went straight home and made himself a unicycle. In three weeks he mastered the tricky wheel. In 1910 a theatrical promoter saw Walter exhibiting his skill at an Odd Fellow's parade, and signed him up for a vaudeville act. He was billed as "The Boy Wonder." "The World's Master Unicyclist, and a "Loose Nut on Wheels." In those early days he met with over 200 falls, usually into the orchestra pit.

Above left:
**WALTER NILSSON, STAR OF
"HELLZ-A-POPPIN"**
This photo shows Nilsson wearing his
theatrical costume on a Star bicycle.
Courtesy of Walter Nilsson

Above right:
**JACK NATIRBOFF —
THE BICYCLE CLOWN**
Courtesy of Jack Natirboff

Bottom right:
**JOE JACKSON —
THE CYCLING TRAMP**
Ice Capades of 1943
Courtesy of Joe Jackson

WALTER SHYRETTO
Courtesy the New York Radio City Music Hall

In 1933-34, he rode his eight-foot-high unicycle from New York to San Francisco 3,386 miles in 117 days on a wager. He was pictured by Ripley in *Believe It or Not.* Nilsson was the only one who could mount his eight-foot unicycle from the ground without the use of a ladder. He also invented a "walk-o-cycle made from bicycle gears, a brace of old wooden legs and a second-hand pair of shoes.

In 1938, he was booked for a long run in Olsen and Johnson's Broadway review "Hellzapoppin" at the New York Winter Garden. This brought him fame and he toured Europe with his unicycle. At his home in Closter, New Jersey he had a collection of over 400 bicycles, many of his own invention. One summer he exhibited his odd machines at Coney Island, selling rides to the public at his "Funi-Cycle" pavillion.

I met Walter Nilsson after a show at the Winter Garden. Walter and his wife were very hospitable and there were always bicyclist friends visiting his museum on weekends. He gave me a first lesson in unicycling. Walter Nilsson's unicycle was promised to the American

Bicycle Hall of Fame Museum at Richmondtown, New York City.

The illustration shows Walter wearing his theatrical costume on a Star bicycle.

Walter Shyretto

Walter hails from Germany. When quite young he joined a bicycle club and became interested in artistic cycling. He also interested his brother Alfred and sister Hanny in the unicycle. They acted as a threesome on the stage for some years.

Walter performs an act in which he appears as a suave and neatly groomed gentleman in a top hat and cane. He pedals to music and also does a daring drunk routine awheel.

He has presented his unique act in Germany, Italy, Russia and England. The act was well received at the Follies Bergere in Paris. I saw him twice at Radio City Music Hall.

A critic has called his act "a Joe Jackson with sex."

The Remarkable Romanos

This artistic cycling family--Tony, Helene and Patrick Romano--came to America from France in 1952. They performed in a specialty bicycle act entitled "The World on Wheels," touring America and Canada with The Ice Capades.

Father Tony was a former gymnast and high-wire performer. He has designed and built all the various bicycles use in the act. The highlight of the act is the agility and balancing skill of Tony Romano, who amazes audiences by riding a four and half inch bike, while his family rests atop his shoulders.

They have toured the world, appearing on stages in five continents and on television. At Las Vegas they performed in several hotels. They've made guest appearances on the Ed Sullivan, Gary Moore, Johnny Carson and Steve Allen television shows.

They travel with The Ice Capades in a large custombuilt mobile home in which they enjoy real home-cooked meals. "The Romanos' world revolves on tiny wheels."

83

Top:
PALLEN'S BEARS
Photo by Al Hatos
Courtesy of the Sells-Floto Circus

At left:
THE MARQUIS CHIMPS
Courtesy of Gene Detroy

84

The Volantes
Two Started with One and Won

Don Thompson and Scott Beldin were both born and raised in Portland, Oregon. While in grade school they became members of a tumbling team. The newly formed team performed for the Parent-Teacher Association; with the proceeds they purchased a unicycle. After several weeks practice (including bumps and scrapes) they learned to ride the tricky wheel. They soon graduated to eight-foot machines. Now the "Uni-Kids" performed at local 4-H Banquets, P.T.A. events and picnics. Scott learned to play the accordian and Don learned to ride the unicycle with Scott on his shoulders playing the accordian.

After four years they decided to turn professional. They called themselves "The Volantes." They met Eddie Cochran who became their manager and agent. He equipped the team with custom-made, lightweight, well-balanced portable cycles.

The Volantes have performed before supper clubs, theaters, fairs and television in America and Europe, including the famous Lido Cafe in Paris. These two enterprising American kids are on their way to the very top in show business on wheels.

Karl Wallenda

Karl was the founder and director of "The Great Wallendas" one of the most daring high wire acts known.

He began his circus career as a catcher in a trapeze number. Karl soon developed his own high wire act. He advertised for a girl to join his troupe and found Helen Kreis, who later became his wife.

The troupe joined the Ringling Brothers Barnum and Bailey Combined Shows. His most dazzling feat was riding bicycles to form a human pyramid. The Wallendas always performed in mid-air without a net.

On March 22, 1978 Karl gave his last high wire performance. He fell from a wire stretched between two hotels in Puerto Rico. High winds caused the veteran to lose his balance. The world mourned his passing.

The Marquis Chimps

A Manchester Englishman named Detroy originated the chimp act. He started with three chimps. "Charlie" (female) ten years old, "Enoch" (male) aged eight, and baby "Candy" aged two. They cost from $1,000 to $1,500 each and came from Equatorial Africa. Their life span is about 60 years. Chimps have a nine-month pregnancy, and they can catch a severe cold from a human.

These funny chimpanzees have an income of about $250,000 a year, but prefer bananas to cash. They catch onto a new act very quickly and are encouraged to perform with a reward of jelly beans. One of their most difficult tricks is riding a unicycle.

They have appeared at the New York Palace, Radio City Music Hall and at the Desert Inn at Las Vegas. "Monkey Business Pays Off."

Pallens Bears—Sells-Floto Circus

About the turn of the century a circus was traveling around Holland. It gave a performance in a small town. A young Dutch girl attended the show and met the trainer of the bears. They fell in love and spent the night together. The father of the girl suggested to his daughter that she marry her hero, the bear trainer, and she did.

She then spent her life seeing the world from a circus tent. Trainer Pallenberg taught his new bride the secret of handling and training the bears. A lifetime of training genius went into this bicycling and skating bear act. They were very difficult tricks for the animals to master.

After touring Europe for many years, they came to America and joined the Sells-Floto Circus. In the 1920's their act was given top billing. They also gave performances at the Atlantic City Hamid Pier Show.

The Story of the King Charles Troupe

"The razzle-dazzle hijinks of the King Charles Troupe has, in the space of a few years, become one of the most talked of features of the Ringling Brothers Barnum and Bailey's Combined Shows, Inc. Delightfully displaying their unicycle expertise, the group joins forces for the wildest, most uninhibited basketball game ever--and it's on wheels.

"The young men in the troupe hail from the Bronx, New York. They have an absolutely marvelous time working with the circus, a fact which is obvious to their delighted audiences."

The author, as amateur coach of cycling at the Theodore Roosevelt High School in New York City, was an early sponsor of a part of this unique act. Several of the professional performers started their careers as members of this school act. The youthful performers obtained their first tests of show business when they presented a fast-moving unicycle show to 2,000 of their fellow students at a special assembly program.

It gives me great satisfaction to know that his little amateurs have now risen to big-time show business.

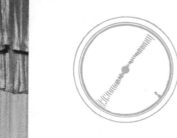

Facing page
Top left:
THE WALLENDAS
The late indomitable Karl Wallenda, who brought his group of aerialists to circuses around the world, stands on a chair balanced on a bar held by Tino Wallenda, a grandson (left), and Luis Murillo, a Chilean high wire expert. They are seated on bicycles based on a 3/4 inch cable high above the ground. Awaiting arrival of the entourage is Ricky Bogino Wallenda, another grandson.
Courtesy of Karl Wallenda

Top right:
THE REMARKABLE ROMANOS
Courtesy of the New York Radio City Music Hall

Bottom left:
THE VOLANTES
"Two Started With One and Won"
Courtesy of Eddie Cochran

Bottom right:
STEVEN McPEAK
Here he is riding the tallest unicycle in the world — 31 feet, 2 inches — February 2, 1969 at Circus, Circus, Las Vegas, Nevada.
Courtesy of Steven McPeak

This page:
THE KONDOVI TROUPE — HIGH WIRE CYCLISTS
Courtesy RINGLING BROTHERS BARNUM AND BAILEY COMBINED SHOWS INC.

Great Bicycle Films

Director Vittorio De Sica
The Bicycle Thief

Director DeSica began his theatrical career in Italy in 1923. After serving in the army he decided on an acting career. A popular singer of Neapolitan ballads, he jumped to the screen and made his debut in 1931. From Director Mario Camperini he learned motion picture techniques.

"The Bicycle Thief" was first shown in New York at the World 49 Street Theater in January 1950.

The story of this great bicycle film is based on a novel, *Bicycle Thieves* by Bartolini.

"The Bicycle Thief" is the story of a poor bill poster, whose bicycle is stolen. He hunts frantically to recapture it. He must find the bicycle to hold down his job, his family depends on him, and the loss of the bicycle is a severe economic blow.

The picture was shot on location in Rome. The leading players are non-professionals. The film required eight months of preparation and eight months of actual filming. It won the Brussels Film Festival grand prize, the American Academy Award and many other prizes. The New York Film Critics voted it "Best Foreign Film of the Year." The New York Herald Tribune wrote, "It is a brilliant and unforgetable motion picture."

Bonita Granville and Jane Powell
Song of the Open Road

This charming story of youth hosteling on bicycles in California in the 1940's begins with the girls, Bonita Granville and Jane Powell who are tired of city life, and invite friends to join them on a hosteling weekend, pedaling along the open road. They ride along the palm-lined highways singing "Rollin' Down the Road," "Fun in the Sun," "Delightfully Dangerous," "Too Much in Love" and "Here It Is Monday." At the hostel they earn their keep by picking oranges and doing odd repair jobs.

In the evening the happy cyclists are entertained by Edgar Bergen, W. C. Fields, Sammy Kaye and Orchestra. It was a wonderful adventure for the young people.

The picture was produced by Charles R. Rogers and directed by S. Sylvan Simon. The cycling song hits were by Walter Kent and Kim Gannon. Other music in the production was by George Dobbs.

Released through United Artists.

Joe E. Brown
Six Day Bike Rider

This great American screen and stage comic was born in Holgate, Ohio in 1892. The neighbors of Mathias and Ann Brown were sorry to see the Brown's fourth child, Joe, cursed with such an enormous mouth; but that very feature zoomed him to the top of the screen's funny men.

As a youth he was a gymnast, acrobat, ball and polo player. In 1915, he married and had two sons, one of whom was killed in World War II. Joe died at the age of 80 in Los Angeles, California. During his life, Joe E. Brown made over 50 films, of which "Six Day Bike Rider" was one of his finest.

The film was produced by First Nation Pictures, Inc. and shown at the Rialto Theater in New York in November 1934. In this film Joe plays Wilfred Simpson, a smalltown boy longing to win the love of the village sweetheart, Phyllis Jenkins, played by Maxine Doyle.

Wilfred (Joe) decides to become a six day bicycle champion in order to impress Phyllis. He starts training and is caught in a series of predicaments that make for a funny picture. After many spills and thrills, with much slapstick and suspense, the hero wins the big race in the end. In the finale Joe rides around the track with his girl riding the handle bars.

A news reporter wrote, "Six Day Bike Rider" is one of Joe E. Brown's brightest and most hilarious comedies." The story and screen play was by Earl Baldwin and the movie was directed by Lloyd Bacon.

Interesting Bicycle Stunts

Blondin, about 1860, pedalled his boneshaker bicycle across Niagara Falls on a wire. Mark Twain referred to him as "that adventuresome ass."

Thomas Godwin of Great Britain rode 75,065 miles in the year 1939.

M. Owens, of Jackson Hole, Wyoming, was the first to pedal his high-wheel around Yellowstone National Park in 1885. His bicycle is on exhibition at the Madison Station Museum.

Tony Piso of the Century Road Club Association of New York rode across the United States handcuffed to his bicycle to stimulate U. S. Navy recruiting in 1917.

Dare-Devil Shreyer rode his bicycle down an inclined plane and landed in a pool of water at Coney Island. He missed the tank only once. In 1902 composer Tonnele wrote a song in his honor entitled "Dare-Devil."

Yale University Bicycle Club members conducted a bicycle race from New Haven to Poughkeepsie, drinking a liter of beer in route at designated stops. They all finished the tour and were greeted at Poughkeepsie by the Vassar girls with hugs and kisses.

M. Robertson, of Washington, D.C., rode his Star bicycle (with small wheel in front instead of rear) down the capitol steps without a mishap.

Editor Bill Jenack, of the Unicycling Society of America, taught a blind man to ride a unicycle; the man later gave fancy riding performances.

Steven McPeak rode from Chicago to Las Vegas—over 2,000 miles—on a unicycle. He also holds the record for pedalling a high unicycle over 32 feet in height. He married Connie Fullerton on a high wire. He is the "king of the Modern Unicyclists."

Harry H. Kramer, of Greenville, South Carolina, at the age of 75, gave unicycling exhibitions in Estes Park, Colorado in 1935.

Walter Nilsson, the unicycle star of the Broadway show "Hellzapoppin," won a $10,000 wager by riding his high unicycle across the United States in 1934.

THE KING CHARLES TROUPE
Basketball bravado and bicycling virtuosity combine to make the Troupe one of many unique attractions in the 108th Edition of Ringling Brothers Barnum and Bailey Circus.
Courtesy of THE RINGLING BROTHERS BARNUM AND BAILEY COMBINED SHOWS INC.

LOVE ON BICYCLES 1869

6
THE COMPOSERS

OVER 400 POEMS ON CYCLING WERE COMposed during the 1880's and 1890's.

Dr. Walter G. Kendall wrote a much-favored poem recalling the pleasures of cycling at a moderate pace. He was a captain of the Boston Bicycle Club for 52 years; quite a record.

Karl Kron (whose real name was Lyman Hotchkiss Bagg) wrote "Velocipede" while a Yale student in 1869. He begged for road rights for the cyclists of the era. Kron also wrote *Ten Thousand Miles on a Bicycle*. The costs of printing this book were paid for by hundreds of American cyclists whose names are mentioned in the volume.

In 1884 Charles E. Pratt, a founder of the League of American Wheelmen, wrote "A Song of the Wheel." He was a prolific author with interesting articles published in *The Wheelmen* magazine.

The poets' message to the world is "Ride a Bicycle and Be Happy."

Dr. Walter G. Kendall

This active and honored American bicyclist was born in Woburn, Massachusetts and graduated from Boston Dental College in 1880.

He was a founder member of the famous old Boston Bicycle Club, the first cycling club in America. Kendall was their elected Captain for 52 years, a most unusual honor in the world of cycling.

For over 50 years he led the annual "Wheel Around the Hub," a tour around the city of Boston. Some years ago some veteran members of the Boston Bicycle Club made the tour in motor cars, most of them being in their high eighties and nineties.

"Doc", as he was affectionately called, was a collector of antique bicycles and cycling memorabilia. Dr. Kendall was also a dog breeder; his animals won 275 first prizes at the dog shows of America. His third hobby was horticulture.

Death overtook this grand old veteran in 1946 at the age of 90.

Bicycle Poetry

The Men Who Ride For Fun

We're the healthy, happy heathen, the Men Who Ride for Fun,
The faithful friends of bicycling, that sport surpassed by none.
We've ridden through long seasons past; we'll ride long seasons more;
And while we've gained both health and strength, we have had fun galore.

We're close to Mother Nature, and she greets us every year
With blossoming flowers, budding trees and sunny atmosphere.
We hear her voice low-calling, just as soon as spring's begun.
She tells her choicest secrets to the Men Who Ride for Fun.

We start the season's wheeling when the frost first leaves the ground.
We know the roads in every town for fifty miles around.
Our minds are clear, our hearts are light, digestion Number One.
We've three big appetites a day, the Men Who Ride for Fun.

There are men who ride for exercise and men who ride for health.
There are men who ride for mileage and men who ride for speed,
And once men rode for fashion, but they quickly petered out.
And are giving their attention now to nervousness and gout.

There are men who ride for mileage and men who ride for speed,
And in a few short seasons they get all the wheel they need
While we keep on year after year; our wheeling's never done.
We hearty, hungry vagabonds, the Men Who Ride for Fun.

We wear each other's burdens and enjoy each other's jokes;
Respect each other's feelings and the rights of other folks.
Bring out your wheels and join us. You'll be welcome, every one,
To the Brothers of the Bicycle, the Men Who Ride for Fun.

Dr. Walter G. Kendall
(Captain of the Boston Bicycle Club for 52 years)

A Song of the Wheel.

Come with me out into the road, my wheel.-
    Out into the road, ere the sun goes down!
Thy hoofs of round rubber and ribs of true steel
    Shall bear me away from this tiresome town.

Aloft on thy saddle, set safe from all harm,-
    The saddle ne'er mounted by trouble or care,-
I'll hie me away where the woodlands yet charm,
    Where valleys are smiling and fields are yet fair.

With feet on thy quick-moving pedals impressed,-
    The pedals that speed from the hurrying street,-
I'll seek the calm hills and the landscapes at rest,
    Where green leaves are fresh and the breezes are sweet.

Out over the road while the sun is yet high,
  While sunlight and shadows are nimbly at play,-
O Bicycle! free as the swallows that fly,
  We'll hover, we'll hasten, as joyful as they.

Charles E. Pratt
(Founder of the League of American Wheelmen)

A Morning Ride

Up with the lark in the first flush of morning,
  Ere the world wakes to its work or its play;
Off for a spin to the wide stretching country,
  Far from the close, stifling city away.

A spring to the saddle, a spurt with the pedal,
  The roadway is flying from under my wheel.
With motions so sprightly, with heart beating lightly,
  How glorious to master this creature of steel!

Now mounting the hill-slope with slow, steady toiling,
  Each turn of the wheel brings us nearer the goal,
And so on life's journey 'tis patient endeavor
  That opens the path to the conquering soul.

As we mount the last hill, to the smoke clouded city,
  Just beginning to boil with its great human tide,
It calls us to toil, and to enter the conflict -
  So endeth this morning our twenty mile ride.

The Wheelman 1883
(Composed Yesteryear but True Today)

To Arcady
(With the Wheelmen of the Gay Nineties)

What men are you who
  The dusty road this summer day,
Riding together, twenty strong
  Up hill and down in bold array,
As in the times of Border fray
  Knights of the whirring wheel are we
And wither are ye wending, pray?
  We are on the road to Arcady.

Merry cyclists that, with song
  And laughter, pedal onward say
How, in a world where chains go wrong,
  Where tyres collapse, and screws give way,
Ye still can be so blithe and gay
  Are all your duns at rest, that ye
Can sing and laugh so lightly? Nay
  We are on the road to Arcady.

William Weaver Tomlinson
(Composed about 1895)

The Old Timer

In a high and lonely attic, where the cobwebs weave and twine
  As the dusty evening sun comes creeping in,
Reclines an ancient relic which was once a pride of mine
  Though now, alas! displaced by modern kin.
'Tis an old and rusty bicycle of inches fifty-two,
With tiny ribbling trailer wheel behind,
And its ruddy rubber tires to-day are ragged through and through,
  Its dangling hub-lamp many seasons blind,
In that high and lonely attic, full many a year ago,
  I put that ancient bicycle to rest,
I laid it up in lavender of memories - who shall know
  The journeys that it ventured, or their quest
O, the hopes that have been gilded and the hopes that died too soon,
  The fortunes that we made ere we grew old,
The ardent youth that pedalled through the joyous days of June,
  When every gloomy cloud was lined with gold!

Anonymous

Cupid's Tandem

The pedals flew, the rubber run
Spun round and on. The very brim
Of summer's joy flowed full and sweet
For two young hearts that throbbing beat
And cupids fluttering wings were spread
Where swift their tandem sprang and sped
With quickening breath and shining eyes
He saw the glowing color rise
In waves upon her rounded cheek
He bent his head close down to speak
Four words that only lovers know,
He whispered low — "I love you so."

From *Outing* 1898

Her Ruling Passion.
Air—We Wont Go Home Till Morning.

She was dainty, she was pretty,
  Quite a number thought her witty,
And she entertained expensively and
  charmingly, I'm told.
Luncheons, teas and dinner-dances
Incomplete were without Frances;
Countless fellows made advances
For her hand-likewise her gold.
  But, alas! she took to wheeling,
  And it stirred up quite a feeling

'Mongst her beaux, to whom of nothing
   save her bicycle she'd speak,
She said, "I cannot stand 'em,
   Their dismissals I will hand 'em!
And she left home on a tandem
With a clerk at ten per week.

From *Brooklyn Life*

A Fair Cycler.
Air—Haste to the Wedding.
See her spin down the street,
Natty from head to feet,
Saucy, bewitching, sweet,
   Gay as a linnet!
By all the gods! but I'd Mightily like to ride
By that fair cycler's side
   Just for a minute!

Ah! what nymphean grace!
What a poise! what a pace!
Surely, were she to race,
   She could win medals!
Gown trim, yet flowing free,
Hat what a hat should be,
Boots pressing prettily
   Down on the pedals.

Presto! the vision's gone,
Passed like the blush of dawn;
Seem from the scene withdrawn
   Love, light and laughter.
Bless me! how glum I feel!
By Jove! I'll get my wheel,
Mount in a trice, and steal
   Speedily after!

Irving Gilmore
Buffalo Express

On a Tandem.
Air—Annie Laurie.
'Twas the time of meadow lilies,
   And of bobolinks in tune,
When I went to ride with Phyllis
   On a breezy afternoon.
How her jaunty gown became her,
   With her maiden cheeks aglow!
Had I then been asked to name her
   I'd have called her "apple-blow."

As she spoke with blush and dimple
   Of her girlish hopes and fears,
As I watched the sunny rimple
   Of the curls about her ears,
A great wave I could not master
   Through my veins began to steal,
And my heart went whirring faster
   Than the whirring of the wheel.

All too soon the moments fleeted,
   All too swiftly sank the sun;
Fate the love-web had completed
   When at last the goal was won.
Tender were the words between us
   As we stood there side by side,
For the wily son of Venus
   Had been with us on our ride.

Irving Gilmore
New York Sun

Bicycle Bells.
Air—The Valley Lay Smiling.
In the morning all dewy and gray;
A nymph from the gardens Elysian, She dashes and
flashes away!
Past meadows and groves, where the singing
   Of birds all melodious swells,
My heart hears the silvery ringing
   Of the beautiful bicycle bells!

She's a bicycle, bicycle girl,
With hair of the loveliest curl;
She's fresher than clover,
My heart she rides over—
She's a bicycle, bicycle girl!

Her cheeks with the crimson is glowing—
   With all that the rose could impart; The breeze—the
mad wanton!—is blowing
   A kiss and a curl to my heart!
Past meadows where wild birds are winging
   Their way o'er velvety dells,
She glides with a ravishing ringing
   Of the silvery bicycle bells!

Philadelphia Times

What Fellow Would Not Dare.
Air—Love's Young Dream.
Was ever life so sweet, love,
Were ever nights so fair,
Were ever stars so bright, love,
What fellow would not dare
To win a stolen kiss, love,

94

THE FAMILY OUTING
Drawn by Dalrymple

When riding by the mile?
For love is sweet and lips are near—
Since tandems are the style.

Were roses half so sweet, love,
Were kisses half so rare
As one dear kiss from you, love,
What fellow would not dare
To pedal on forever,
With a burden half so dear?
A trust he ne'er would sever—
A-wheeling in the rear.

So steal away the kisses,
While hearts and lips are young,

When hid are life's abysses,
Before one's tires are sprung.
There's naught in after dreaming—
No memories half so dear,
As in the moon's white gleaming—
A-wheeling in the rear.

M. Ware Johnson
Detroit Free Press

THE BLOOMER GIRL AND ESCORT
Drawn by Ehrhart 1896

Ned and Sue.

Air—When ye Gang awa,' Jamie.

Along the country road came Sue;
  Her heart was very sore at Ned;
Not far behind came Edward, too,
  Not knowing Sue was on ahead.

That morning they had fallen out,
  And both rushed forth to take a spin.
They knew not what 'twas all about,
  But both knew what it ended in.

Now Sue a hedge is passing by;
  Alas, her tire is punctured there!
She halts beside the road to try
  To fill the flattened tube with air.

Then Ned comes wheeling bravely on—
  A thorn waylays his tire, too;
And soon with wind and patience gone,
  He halts across the way from Sue.

Alack, he finds with sinking heart
  That far behind he's left his pump!
He can't retreat, he cannot start,
  Now surely he is up a stump.

When, lo, across the dusty road
  The gentle girl who sees his plight
Comes tripping with her pump; the load
  Slips from his heart and out of sight.

A look, a thought, a spoken word,
  A hasty pumping in of air,
The tender singing of a bird,
  And only peace is smiling there.

Along the country road came Sue,
  Her heart at Ned no longer sore,
And by her side rode Edward, too.
  And now they quarrel nevermore.

New York World

That Bloomer Girl

That bloomer girl -
  She's modest as a rosebud rare
  And lithe her action as she glides
  Down the hills, or smoothly rides
  With zephyrs breathing thru her hair
  That bonnie bloomer girl.

That bloomer girl -
  And oft the boys will pause and sigh;
  She holds them with her magic grace
  The blushing sweetness of her face
  A lovely vision fleeting by
  That dainty bloomer girl.

That bloomer girl - With lithesome heart she takes her
way
  And may she ever feel as free,
  And life run smooth and joyously,
  As those glad eyes reveal today
  That winsome bloomer girl.

A. Stainforth

To a Weeping Bloomerette

She sits by the roadside weeping,
  A maiden fair to see
And only her wheel is keeping
  Her company 'neath the tree

What ails the maiden I wonder
  What's the cause of her dreadful woe
And why is she sitting under
  That tree, I should like to know,

She has claimed that her sex is equal
  To the other in all respects
And this is her painful sequel
  Throwing light on her own defects

For her grief there's a sad sad reason
  See how badly she seems to feel
She has ridden this whole long season
  Yet she cannot repair her wheel

And the reason she sits lamenting
  Well the cause is a nail or brier
And she knows not the art of cementing
  Or of plugging a punctured tire.

Charles Murphy
Dedicated to the new fashionable bloomer girls of 1896

Saved

A bloomer girl
  Just left her wheel;
A lurking piece
  Of orange peel.

A careless step,
  A sudden slip
A scream, a fall
  A fatal rip

A man at hand
  With mackintosh,
A garment just
  The thing begosh!

The bloomer girl
  Raised from the ground,
The garment wrapped
  Her form around.

A store at hand;
  The maid has gone;
All's over and
  The band plays on.

Chicago Times Herald

The Masculine Wish.

O for some other land than this, in any
　　sort of zone,
Where females still are females, where
　　new women are unknown!
Where the eternal fitness of all things
　　there's naught to jar!
Where women wear no clothes of men,
　　their forms divine to mar!
Where clinging robes are still the style,
　　as in the long ago,
'Till bicycles brought pantaloons and
　　plunged us into woe!
May some new Moses lead us soon to
　　that thrice-blessed shore,
Where the bloomers cease from bloom-
　　ing and the panties pant no more!

Chas. J. Colton
New Orleans Times-Democrat

The Copper and the Scorcher.
Air—The Wearing of the Green.

He was a mounted copper,
　　Upon an iron steed,
And was laying for the scorcher,
　　Who rode at lawless speed;
When whizzing 'round the corner,
　　At a breakneck, lightning pace,
Appeared a reckless rider,
　　Whereupon the cop gave chase.

"I say there!" cried the bluecoat,
　　As he humped himself about,
"You're arrested for fast riding."
　　When the scorcher heard the shout
He looked o'er his shoulder,
　　And he didn't do a thing
But pedal all the harder
　　And make the welkin ring.

"I like that," said the "finest,"
　　As through the thoroughfare
He started for his victim;
　　And the crowd that gathered there
Cheered the racer, jeered the copper
　　And wagered ten to one
On the scorcher as he sped along
　　On that exciting run.

In and out among the horses
　　And wagons on the street
They dodged about most artfully,

Doing many a dangerous feat;
But the bluecoat was outdistanced,
　　He set too slow a pace,
And his anger gave expression
　　In the wrath upon his face.

At last grown weak and weary,
　　The copper swore he'd shoot,
And reached back for his pistol,
　　But the crowd cried, "Don't, you brute!"
But he aimed it at the scorcher,
　　If he didn't, I'm a liar;
"Bang!" and the scorcher tumbled,
　　For the cop had pierced his tire.

Washington Times.

A Sight

I saw a girl
Amid the whirl,
She'd golden hair,
Her face was fair,
Her garments fair,
Her form divine,
　　With eyes like stars.

She rode a bike
and such a sight!
She drove her steed
At scorchers' speed,
Her back was humped,
Her head near bumped
　　The handle bars.

Buffalo Courier

The Scorcher

The scorcher tore full furiously
　　Along the busy street,
Unmindful of the obstacles
That he perchance might meet,
He scorned to heed the warning cries,
　　That record-breaking chump
And he ran plump on a coal cart
　　Now his wheel is on the dump.

Philadelphia North American

98

THE SCORCHERS
Drawn by Syd Griffin

Scorching

Sing a song of scorching,
  Hip pocket full of rye;
Four and twenty little nips
  Taken on the sly.
When the run was over
  His head began to spin.
Wasn't this a pretty state
  To go a-wheeling in?

The host was in the roadway,
  Inflating a new tire;
The hostess wabbling in the ditch,
  Bestrewn with dust and mire;
The daughter struggling with her chain,
  All tangled with her clothes;
Our scorcher runs to aid her
  And tumbles on his nose.

New York World

TAKING A HEADER OR OVER THE HANDLES

Scorchers.

Three scorchers went hustling down the street,
  Along the street, as the sun went down;
As if they were trying a record to beat.
  And the "coppers" were chasing them out of town;
For fools must scorch, and fools must hump,
And the less of a rider, the more of a chump,
  And they leave their victims groaning. Three corpses
lay out on the pavement there,
  In the tracks of the wheels that the scorchers rode,
And the ambulance came with a dash and a swear,
  And jounced away with its ghastly load;
But the fools still ride, and the fools still hump,
Who ought to be run out of town on the jump,
  And the people will cease their groaning.

Karl H. Wisewell
Rochester Democrat and Chronicle.

Over the Handles

One day I was riding my wheel so free
  Toward the garden wall
A charmer was standing and looking at me
  From over the garden wall
Her face was so fair,
  So saucy her air,
I was rattled completely,
  And right there and then
I took a bad header
  And flew through the air
Over the garden wall

Chorus

Over the garden wall
  A terrible, terrible fall,
I never did yet
  A header get
Which filled my soul
  With such regret,
As the time I struck
  Head first in the wet
Over the garden wall.

The Wheelman, 1882

A Header

Going leg after leg,
  (As the dog went to Dover)
When he came to a stone,
  Down he went over.

Lyra Bicyclical, 1880

Those Ordinary Days

The man hopped on his high bicycle,
  And all around him fled,
His front wheel struck a cobble stone -
  They picked him up for dead,
They scraped the mud from off his clothes,
  And soon he began to holler;
He swore off riding that machine -
  And sold it to another feller.

Anonymous 1895

Books

High Road and Lonning, John Helston, Philip Allan, London, 1898.
Humors of Cycling, Jerome K. Jerome and others, Chatto and Windus, London, 1905.
Legends of the Wheel, Arthur Waugh, London, 1898.
Lyra Bicyclica: 40 Poets of the Wheel, J.G. Dalton, Boston, 1880.
Lyra Cyclus: The Wheel, Edmund Redwood, Rochester, New York, 1897.
Over the Handles: Cycling Sketches: The Wheelmen's Annual, Salem, Massachusetts, 1887.
Mr. Punch Awheel, edited by J.A. Hammerston, Education Books Ltd., London, 1905.
Sixty Poets of the Road, J.G. Dalton, E.C. Hodges, Boston, 1895.

Periodicals

Outing, The Outing Company Ltd., London, 1887.
Outing and The Wheelmen, The Wheelman Co., Boston, 1885.
The Cyclist, London, 1881-1882.
The Hub, George Newnes, London, 1896.
The Wheelmen, The Wheelman Co., Boston, 1882-1884.
The Wheel World, London, 1886.

Bicycle Prose

The Mark Twain Museum and His High Wheel Bicycle

Mark Twain, whose real name was Samuel Langhorne Clemens, was a great American humorist, writer, newspaperman and lecturer. His most famous books were his stories of boyhood life, *Tom Sawyer* and *Huckleberry Finn.*

He was born in Florida, Missouri on November 30th, 1835. In 1839 his family moved to Hannibal on the Mississippi River. This was the setting for many of his novels.

The Mark Twain Museum is located in a building adjoining the boyhood home. The exhibits include his typewriter, corn cob pipe, favorite chair, letters, pictures, books etc. In the center of the room stands his old high-wheel bicycle, which is in good condition and about which he wrote this whimsical essay. I visited the museum on a recent bicycle tour to the national parks. Mark Twain lets the reader guess whether he ever mastered riding the high-wheel.

The following abridged essay, "Taming the Bicycle" has been reproduced through the courtesy of the publishers, Harper and Row of New York. It is from the book *What is Man.* It is the personal story of his struggles with a high-wheel about the year 1884. History does not tell if he conquered it.

THE MARK TWAIN BICYCLE, HOME AND MUSEUM AT HANNIBAL, MISSOURI

Taming the Bicycle

"I thought the matter over, and concluded I could do it. So I went down and bought a barrel of Pond's Extract and a bicycle. The Expert came home with me to instruct me. We chose the back yard, for the sake of privacy, and went to work.

Mine was not a full-grown bicycle, but only a colt - a fifty-inch, with the pedals shortened up to forty-eight - and skittish, like any other colt. The Expert explained the thing's points briefly, then he got on its back and rode around a little, to show me how easy it was to do. He said that dismounting was perhaps the hardest thing to learn, and so we would leave that to the last. But, he was in error there. He found, to his surprise and joy, that all he needed to do was to get me on the machine and stand out of the way: I could get off, myself. Although I was wholly inexperienced, I dismounted in the best time on record. He was on that side shoving up the machine; we all came down with a crash, he at the bottom, I next, and the machine on top.

We examined the machine, but it was not in the least injured. This was hardly believable. Yet the Expert assured me that it was true; in fact the examination proved it. I was partly to realize, then, how admirably these things are constructed. We applied some Pond's Extract, and resumed. The Expert got on the other side to shove up this time, but I dismounted on that side; so the result was as before.

The machine was not hurt. We oiled ourselves up again, and resumed. This time the Expert took up a sheltered position behind, but somehow or other we landed on him again.

He was full of surprised admiration; said it was abnormal. She was all right, not a scratch on her, not a timber started anywhere. I said it was wonderful while we were greasing up, but he said that when I came to know these steel spider-webs I would realize that nothing

102

but dynamite could cripple them. Then he limped out to a position, and we resumed once more. This time the Expert took up the position of shortstop, and got a man to shove up behind. We got up a handsome speed, and presently traversed a brick, and I went out over the top of the tiller and landed, head down, on the instructor's back, and saw the machine fluttering in the air between me and the sun. It was well it came down on us, for that broke the fall, and it was not injured.

Five days later I got out and was carried down to the hospital, and found the Expert doing pretty fairly. In a few more days I was quite sound. I attribute this to my prudence in always dismounting on something soft. Some recommend a feather bed, but I think an Expert is better.

The Expert got out at last, brought four assistants with him. It was a good idea. These four held the graceful cobweb upright while I climbed into the saddle; then they formed in column and marched on either side of me while the Expert pushed behind; all hands assisted at the dismount.

The steps of one's progress are distinctly marked. At the end of each lesson he knows he has acquired something, and he also knows what that something is, and likewise that it will stay with him. It is not like studying German, where you mull along, in a groping, uncertain way, for thirty years; and at last, just as you think you've got it, they spring the subjunctive on you and there you are. No - and I see now, plainly enough, that the great pity about the German language is, that you can't fall off it and hurt yourself. There is nothing like that feature to make you attend strictly to business. But I also see, by what I have learned of bicycling, that the right and only sure way to learn German is by the bicycling method. That is to say, take a grip on one villainy of it at a time, and learn it - not ease up and shirk to the next, leaving that one half learned.

When you have reached the point in bicycling where you can balance the machine tolerably fairly and propel it and steer it, then comes your next task - how to mount it. You do it in this way: you hop along behind it on your right foot, resting the other on the mounting-peg, and grasping the tiller with your hands. At the word you rise on the peg, stiffen your left leg, hang your other one around in a general and indefinite way, lean your stomach against the rear of the saddle, and then fall off, maybe on one side, maybe on the other, but you fall off. You get up and do it again; and once more; and then several times.

By this time you have learned to keep your balance; and also to steer without wrenching the tiller out by the roots (I say tiller because it is a tiller; "handle bar" is a lamely descriptive phrase). So you steer along, straight ahead, a little while, then you rise forward, with a steady strain, bringing your right leg, and then your body, into the saddle, catch your breath, fetch a violent hitch this way and then that, and down you go again.

And now you have come to the voluntary dismount; you learned the other kind first of all. It is quite easy to tell one how to do the voluntary dismount; the words are few, the requirements simple, and apparently undifficult; let your left pedal go down till your left leg is nearly straight, turn your wheel to the left, and get off as you would from a horse. It certainly does sound exceedingly easy; but it isn't. I don't know why it isn't, but it isn't. Try as you may, you don't get down as you do from a horse, you get down as you would from a house afire. You make a spectacle of yourself every time.

During eight days I took a daily lesson of an hour and a half. At the end of this twelve working-hours' apprenticeship I was graduated - in the rough. I was pronounced competent to peddle my own bicycle without outside help. It seems incredible, this celerity of acquirement. It takes considerably longer than to learn horse-back-riding in the rough.

Now it is true that I could have learned without a teacher, but it would have been risky for me, because of my natural clumsiness. The self-taught man seldom knows anything accurately, and he does not know a tenth as much as he could have known if he had worked under teachers; and, besides, he brags, and is the means of fooling other thoughtless people into going and doing as he himself has done. There are those who imagine that the unlucky accidents of life - life's "experiences" - are in some way useful to us. I wish I could find out how. I never knew one of them to happen twice. They always change off and swap around and catch you on your inexperienced side. If personal experience can be worth anything as an education, it wouldn't seem likely that you could trip Methuselah; and yet if that old person could come back here it is more than likely that one of the first things he would do would be to take hold of one of these electric wires and tie himself all up in a knot. Now the surer thing and the wiser thing would be for him to ask somebody whether it is a good thing to take hold of. But that would not suit him; he would be one of those self-taught kind that go by experience; he would want to examine for himself. And he would find, for his instruction, that the coiled patriarch shuns the electric wire; and it would be useful to him, too, and would leave his education in quite a complete and rounded out condition, till he could come again, some day, and go on bouncing a dynamite-can around to find out what was in it. But we wander from the point. However, get a teacher; it saves much time and Pond's Extract.

Before taking final leave of me, my instructor inquired concerning my physical strength, and I was able to inform him that I hadn't any. He said that that was a defect which would make up-hill wheeling pretty difficult for me at first; but he also said the bicycle would soon remove it. The contrast between his muscles and mine were quite marked. He wanted to test mine, so I offered my biceps - which was my best. It almost made him smile. He said, "It is pulpy, soft, and yielding, and rounded; it evades pressure, and glides from under the fingers; in the dark a body might think it was an oyster in a rag." Perhaps this made me look grieved, for he added briskly, "Oh, that's all right; you needn't worry about that; in a little while you can't tell it from a petrified kidney. Just go right along with your practice; you're all right."

Then he left me, and I started out alone to seek adventures. You don't really have to seek them - that is nothing but a phrase - they come to you.

Within the next five days I achieved so much progress that the boy, who was perched on a gate-post, munching a hunk of maple sugar couldn't keep up with me. He had to content himself with watching me fall at long range.

There was a row of low stepping-stones across one end of the street, a measured yard apart, even after I got so I could steer pretty fairly I was so afraid of those stones that I always hit them. They gave me the worst falls I ever got in that street, except those which I got from dogs. I have seen it stated that no expert is quick enough to run over a dog; that a dog is always able to skip out of his way. I think that may be true; but I think that the reason he couldn't run over the dog was because he was trying to. I do not try to run over any dog. But I ran over every dog that came along. I think it made a great deal of difference. If you try to run over the dog he knows how to calculate, but if you are trying to miss him he does not know how to calculate, and is liable to jump the wrong way every time. It was always so in my experience. Even when I could not hit a wagon I could hit a dog that came to see me practice. They all liked to see me practice, and they all came, for there was very little going on in our neighborhood to entertain a dog. It took time to learn to miss a dog, but I achieved even that.

I can steer as well as I want to, now.

Get a bicycle. You will not regret it if you live.

Hints for Biking Beginners

1. Insure your life and limbs. The former will benefit your relations, the latter yourself.

2. Learn on a hired machine. The best plan is to borrow a machine from a friend. It saves hiring. Should the tyre become punctured, the brake be broken, the bell cracked, the lamp missing, and the gear out of gear, you will return it as soon as possible, advising your friend to provide himself with a stronger one next time.

3. Practise on some soft and smooth ground. For example, on a lawn; the one next door for choice. A muddy road, although sufficiently soft, is not recommended—the drawbacks are obvious.

4. Choose a secluded place for practising. It may at first sight appear somewhat selfish to deprive your neighbours of a gratuitous performance which would be certain to amuse them. Nevertheless, be firm.

5. Get someone to hold you on. Engage a friend in an interesting conversation while you mount your bicycle. Do you remember Mr. Winkle's dialogue with Sam Weller when he attempted skating? You can model your conversation on this idea. Friend will support you while you ride and talk. Keep him at it. It will be excellent exercise for him, physically and morally. Also economical for you; as, otherwise, you would have to pay a runner.

6. Don't bike; trike.

Mr. Punch Awheel

Wonders on Wheels

WONDER if my doctor was right in ordering me to take this sort of exercise.

Wonder whether I look very absurd while accepting the assistance of an attendant who walks by my side and keeps me from falling by clutches at my waistbelt.

Wonder whether it would have been better to go to Hyde Park instead of Battersea.

Wonder whether the policeman, the postman, the nurse with the perambulator, the young lady reading the novel, and the deck passengers on the passing steamboat are laughing at me.

Wonder whether I shall keep on now that my attendant has let go.

Wonder whether the leading wheel will keep straight on until we have passed that lamp-post.

Wonder whether the next spill I have will be less painful than the last.

ALL HEIL! POTPOURRI
By E. Kneiss

Wonder why mats are not laid down by the County Council in the roads for the comfort of falling cyclists.

Wonder why the cycle suddenly doubled up and landed me in the gutter.

Wonder whether the pretty girl in the hat, whose face is hidden by a novel, smiled at my misadventure.

Wonder whether the person who has just come to grief over yonder is using good language or words of an inferior quality.

Wonder whether my attendant is right in urging me to remount and have another try.

Wonder whether I look well wobbling.

Wonder whether the elderly spinster with the anxious manner and air of determination is really enjoying herself.

Wonder whether, when I have completed my first hour, I shall want another.

Wonder whether the imp of a boy will run with me.

Wonder whether my second fall in five minutes beats the record.

Wonder, considering the difficulty of progressing half a dozen paces in as many minutes, how those marvellous feats are performed at Olympia.

(By an Old Beginner in *Mr. Punch Awheel*)

Bicycle Songs

During the past century over 150 bicycle songs were composed and published. I have a collection of over 140 song sheets. The two most famous composers are Harry Dacre and Irving Caesar.

Harry Dacre

The most famous bicycle song of all time is "Daisy Bell," or "Bicycle Built for Two."

The composer, Harry Dacre (his real name was Frank Dean or Henry Decker) was an Englishman visiting in New York. He had brought his bicycle with him and the United States custom officer ruled he must pay a duty on the machine. A friend heard the story and replied, "You're lucky it wasn't a bicycle built for two." This gave Harry an idea, he composed a song based on the reply.

Dacre got the popular singer Miss Katie Lawrence to sing the song in a London music hall. It was an instant hit and was sung all over England. It was reported that at the wedding of the Duke of York, the guests danced to the tune.

Its success in America came when Jennie Lindsay sang it at the Atlantic Gardens on the Bowery in New York in 1894. Dacre also composed the sequel song entitled "Fare-You-Well Daisy Bell."

106

Daisy Bell

The Most Popular Bicycle Song of all Time

Chorus

Daisy, Daisy, Give me your answer do
I'm half crazy
All for the love of you
It won't be a stylish marriage
I can't afford a carriage
But you'll look sweet on the seat of a bicycle built for two.

Fare-You-Well Daisy Bell

Chorus

Fare you well Daisy Bell, I will ride alone
Fare you well sweetheart, Thus we have to part
Say good bye, Do not cry
When your lover's gone
Now I mean to have a machine
Especially built for one.

Harry Dacre

The Story of the Bicycle Girl

The girl who was pictured on a music sheet cover, Eva Margaret Gardner, has had a most interesting cycling career.

She designed the bloomer costume she wore. She felt that bloomers were the correct and comfortable attire for women. Later she opened a business as a "Modiste."

Eva was a member of the Pioneer Cycle Club of Brooklyn and won many century medals during her active career. In 1894 she was the first woman to finish the Sag Harbor to Brooklyn run.

Her son Gerard is an active touring cyclist today, and for years rode regularly on Sunday tours of the American Bicycle Touring League. He has been elected to membership on the Board of Governors of The American Bicycle Hall of Fame in New York City.

Chorus
Oh, the bicycle girl, oh the bicycle girl
She's bound, neck or nothing to go;
For she's fast (on the wheel) and in matters of dress
She isn't by any means slow, oh
no, she isn't by any means slow.

Avery Oddfellow and F.W. Meacham

Reference Publications on Bicycle Songs

Books

Handbook of American Sheet Music, J.G. Dalton, Boston, 1880.
Old Sheet Music, Marian Klamkin, Hawthorn Books, New York, 1975.
Song Cycle and Cycle Songs, Garth Groombridge, Perkins-Kent, England, 1930.
Songs of the Wheel, Walter P. Phillips, George Monroe's Sons, New York, 1897.
Wheel Songs, S. Conant Foster, White Stokes and Allen, New York, 1884.

Periodicals

Musigram: Journal of Musical History "Bicycle Songs of Yesterday and Today," Dr. Roland C. Geist, National Sheet Music Society, March 1965.
Transportation in American Songs "Bicycles", Grosvenor Library, Buffalo, New York 1945.

VELOCIPEDE GALOP FOR THE PIANO
By M. F. H. Smith

THE HEROISM OF THE NEW YORK POLICE
By Jay Hambridge 1897

7
THE GAY NINETIES

THE BICYCLE CRAZE DOMINATED THE SPORT activities of America and Europe in the 1890's. Riding a bicycle offered a return to nature, healthy exercise and low cost transportation.

Women were liberated by the bicycle. They no longer had to wear those hampering long skirts but could enjoy the freedom of comfortable and practical bloomers and divided skirts.

Bicycling was pleasant in those days. There were no traffic lights, and very few autos, but there were slow moving carriages. These carriages posed no threat to the cyclists. On group cycling tours many broken down autos

A SAFE CYCLING COURSE FOR THE NOVICE
Drawn by Dalrymple

lined the highways and the bicycle riders often shouted, "Get a Horse!"

The only difficulties the cyclists faced were the miserable condition of the highways with their sharp gravel surface, holes and ruts which were dangerous on wet days. Colonel Pope and the League of American Wheelmen began a "good roads campaign." This resulted in road improvements in many states and started in the state of New Jersey in 1891.

In the 1890's, a great American artist, Frederic Remington, who painted many cycling pictures, wrote to his friend Poultney Bigelow, "I am riding a bike - it is great fun. Everyone in America is riding bikes. It makes the grease come out of a fellow and is the greatest thing to produce a thirst for beer."

At present America is again enjoying a boom in bicycling. I feel, it is a patriotic duty to conserve our energy by using "muscle power."

The Bicycles That People Rode

In 1890, there were over 200 makes of American bicycles on the market. Men rode the diamond frame models and women the drop frame. The racing men rode fixed gears on cycles weighing from 19 to 25 pounds, the tourists rode the heavier coaster brake models with up-bars, weighing from 30 to 40 pounds. Multiple gears did not exist. Equipment included a skirt guard for women and a wide type of saddle. Other sundries included a cyclometer, tool bag, and toe clips.

The first and oldest name in American cycling was the Columbia made by the Pope Manufacturing Company, headed by Colonel Pope himself. The firm has just celebrated it's centenary.

I remember a few trade-marked brands still advertised about 1910. They included, Cleveland, Crescent, Dayton, Elgin, Iver Johnson, Mead, Orient, Pope, Pierce, Racycle, Spalding, Stearns, Tribune, Victor, Wolff-American and Winton. Our champion racers, like Frank Kramer, rode a custom made Pierce, known as the Pierce Kramer Special. The present owner of the Kramer racing bicycle

111

LOVE ON A TANDEM
Drawn by F. M. Howarth

has planned to donate it to the American Bicycle Hall of Fame Museum. It will be a welcome addition to the 35 cycles on display.

During the past eighty years, I have enjoyed riding the following models with few major repairs: Columbia, Crescent, Racycle (two speed model), Iver Johnson, Chater Lea racing, fixed gear model, Schwinn, an English B.S.A. (Birmingham Small Arms) and Moulton, French Peugeot, Austrian Puch, and Italian Frejus.

Where They Cycled in America

New York, Philadelphia, Boston, Chicago, St. Louis, San Francisco and Washington were the leading cities for pleasure cycling during the Nineties. The most popular park areas and cycle paths in New York City were:

Central Park: The circular wide parkway from about 59th Street to 110th Street, which had to be shared with the carriage traffic. This is where the society people of New York called "The Four Hundred" (Mrs. Astor's list) and the elite from the Michaux Cycling Club pedalled. Diamond Jim Brady and Lillian Russell rode both singles and tandem in the park. Another famous tandem couple, Florenz Ziegfeld and Anna Held enjoyed courting days in the park on a bicycle built for two. I saw the Brady-Russell tandem, a few years ago, at the Walter Nilsson Bicycle Museum at Closter, New Jersey. There was still some gold plating left but all the gems had been removed. New York's own Al Smith was reported to have ridden his bicycle from Oliver Street to the Bronx to court his fair lady!

Riverside Drive Cycle Path: This path was from West 97th Street to Grant's Tomb at 120th Street. Thousands rode on this Hudson River path to the old Claremont Inn where riders enjoyed refreshments. Famous Broadway show people who pedalled here included the Barrymores, John and Lionel, and their uncle, John Drew. It was a wide gravel path shaded by old trees and it was just delightful. The New York Bicycle Police patrolled this path; "Mile-a-Minute Murphy" was one of the officers.

THE NEW WOMAN TAKES HER HUSBAND OUT FOR A RIDE
Drawn by Ehrhart

AN AFTERNOON SPIN ON RIVERSIDE DRIVE, NEW YORK

Drawn by W. T. Smedley

The bicycle speed limit was 8 miles an hour. Scorchers were quickly apprehended. As late as 1930, I was stopped by an officer for fast riding on the 130 Street viaduct. The traffic court judge sentenced me to a day in jail or a $2.00 fine. The plea was guilty as charged and a fine was duly paid. A few years later, six of us were enjoying a Sunday morning ride when we were apprehended by the vigilant police and all given summonses and hauled into court. We paid the fine.

The Coney Island Cycle Path: This was a two-lane gravel path extending from Prospect Park to Coney Island, about five and a half miles. The Reverend Henry Ward Beecher was one of the famous riders who enjoyed cycling here. On holidays and weekends, thousands of riders formed a steady stream of riders on their way to cool off at the sea shore. For the racing people and fans there were velodromes at Manhattan Beach and Coney Island.

Boston: Cyclists had a scenic highway along the Charles River and delighful cycling on Cape Cod, Nantucket and Martha's Vineyard. The late Dr. Paul Dudley White cycled from his home daily to attend the Harvard Medical School. Due to his ardent campaign for safe cycling paths, Boston has over 50 miles of paths. Revere Beach had a famous velodrome where the champion class riders, like Kramer, Bald and Taylor competed.

Philadelphia: Cyclists had use of the scenic Schuylkill River Road from the City Hall to the old Strawberry Mansion. At the 1976 Bicentennial, a hundred riders from the Wheelmen paraded through Fairmount Park on high wheels wearing their 1880 attire.

Washington, D.C.: The early riders used the tow path alongside the Chesapeake and Ohio Canal from Georgetown to Cabin John for delightful touring. A few years ago, Supreme Court Justice Douglas officially opened this canal path to the hikers and bikers of the country.

THE FOUR HUNDRED TAKE TO THE BICYCLE
By B. West Clinedinst
A Spring Picture in Central Park

Above

CYCLING IN HYDE PARK, LONDON
By Hal Hurst

Facing page

AU BOIS DE BOULOGNE, PARIS
By Jean Baptiste Guth

Where They Cycled in England

In 1896, English artist Hal Hurst painted a picture of fashionable bicycling in Hyde Park, London. Eight titled riders are shown including Lord and Lady William Nevill, the Countess of Cairns and the Marchioness of Londonderry.

The print appeared in *Vanity Fair* of June 11th, 1896, and the description reads: "The bicycle has become a common object of the Queens highway and the auto has not - yet. The growth of cycling is due to women. The bicycle makers made machines with skirt nets. Today the lady cyclist is as frequent as the man. Cycling pervades London and the country and covers Europe."

It is interesting to note that the English ladies pedalled drop frame models and wore the correct conventional skirt rather than bloomers or divided skirts.

Where They Cycled in France

On June 3, 1897, the French artist Guth sketched twelve members of the French nobility at the Chalet Du Cycle at the Bois de Boulogne. The team of the two bloomer girls were the Contesse Liane de Pougy and the Contesse de Kersaint. The second Contesse had a title dating back to King Charlemagne.

The story of the print from *Vanity Fair* reads in part, "The fashion - which is now becoming a habit - took the world of Paris before that of London. From princesses to commoners, they all ride in Paris. The Bois de Boulogne is filled with "wheels" and bloomers. By the thousands, the cyclists ride forth along the avenues to the Chalets de Cycle by Suresnes. The Parisienne is able to ride a bicycle as well as a man."

Those Early Bicycle Clubs

Over 200 bicycle clubs were organized in the United States in the 1890's and 1900's. The four earliest were, Boston Bicycle Club, February 12th, 1878, Suffolk Bicycle Club (Massachusetts) April 13th, 1878, Bangor Bicycle Club (Maine) September 1st, 1878, and the San Francisco Bicycle Club, November 28th, 1878.

The first bicycle club in England was the Pickwick Cycling Club. The club officers assumed the names of characters in the Dicken's novel.

In America, only three clubs organized in the Nineties are still active today.

The St. Louis Cycling Club: Organized in March 1887. It started as a high wheel group. Activities included both racing and pleasure touring. Among the outstanding members in racing were Carl Schutte, who won a bronze

POSTER FOR THE SPRINGFIELD BICYCLE CLUB TOURNAMENT

Courtesy of the Prints Division, The New York Public Library; Astor, Lenox, and Tilden Foundation

medal in the 1912 Olympics and John Freeman, who was on the 1920 U.S.A. Olympic Road Racing team. I competed for a position on this team, but in vain. Chester Nelson represents this club in racing and Bob Jacoby is their veteran tour leader. Dick Odien, an 1890 rider, writes, "The St. Louis cyclists sing as they lean over the handle bar and they enjoy riding to the fullest." I became an honorary member of the club.

The Century Road Club of America: This club was organized in 1891 in Springfield, Illinois and incorporated in Chicago in 1895. Members have been active in both racing and touring. Two of their popular early leaders were Emile E. Frayzee and Al Everhard. In 1909, Frayzee rode 123 centuries, and a yearly mileage of 23,000. Their famous racing champions include Joe Kopsky, Charley Winter, Fred Spencer and Jack Simes. Veteran coaches include Art Vickery, Dick Swan and Fred Kuhn.

The Century Road Club Association: This racing and touring group was incorporated December 11th, 1899. The charter members included Charles Staubach, Paul Thomas, Dr. LeRoy, and Sylvain Segal. The "Association", as it is known today, has divisions in Long Island, New Haven and Baltimore. At the turn of the century, the racing team of Jensen, Marquart, and the Caldwell Brothers won the Inter-Club Road Racing League Championships. In 1948, Jack Heid was on the U.S.A. Olympic Team, and, in 1967, Sam Zeitlin represented the country at the Pan American Games. Today, the racing teams are coached by Captain Louis Maltese and Frank Bloedel. A few of the cross country records established by members include the New York - St. Louis made by William Winquist, New York-Boston by Vito Cestone, and the New York - Atlantic City by James C. Paul. I joined this club in 1916 and raced on both road and track for four years. In 1919, I was elected club captain, and conducted summer vacation bicycle tours to Niagara Falls, Toronto, Montreal, Boston and Washington. Every year at the annual dinner the veterans meet and talk about "those good old bicycle days at the turn of the century."

Those Grand Old Century Runs

From about 1890 to 1925 the century, or 100 miles in ten hours was a very popular cycling event. The League of American Wheelmen and local cycling clubs promoted these runs. Today, they are again promoted by the League as a national event.

I recall my first official century run in 1916 with the Century Road Club Associastion. These events were held in the spring and fall. There were two divisions, a pleasure group for novices and a fast division for the

racing men. It was a colorful run with each club represented by riders wearing official jerseys. Only Fred Perrault, who came from Boston, wore his 1880 high wheel uniform.

At 7 a.m., the pleasure division riders received their official badges from the run chairman, the bugler sounded off and the riders started in column two formation from Columbus Circle. The badge listed the route and rest stops to Islip, Long Island, the luncheon hour stopover. After a complete 25¢ meal, both pleasure and fast divisions started on the return trip. At Jamaica, the chairman awarded the silver century medals. In 1919, I was the century chairman and had the honor of awarding the medals.

These early runs were quite different from the runs that are held today. All the riders rode fixed gear machines and remained in formation during the entire trip. There was no sprinting permitted. The pleasure division rode at about 12 to 15 miles an hour and the fast riders about 17 to 20 miles an hour. There were practically no autos and no traffic lights to hold up or separate the riders. About 150 riders enjoyed the run, and very few dropped out. Women were not seen on these club runs. Some of the novices came out with 50 to 60 pound machines, called "Klunks." After some 50 miles they usually were tired and returned via train.

These century runs were most enjoyable and everyone felt a sense of achievement. My twenty century medals are cherished possessions.

The New York Sunday Bicycle Trains

Sunday bicycle trains were operated on the Ninth Avenue Elevated Line in the gay nineties. The trains presented a grand opportunity for downtown city cyclists to enjoy a day in the country with their bicycles.

The bicycle car of a train was arranged so that there was a row of seats for riders on one side and racks to hold the bicycles on the opposite side. The train started at Rector Street at 7:30 a.m. and arrived at the destination, 155th Street, at about 8 a.m. The line operated trains in both directions all day.

From 155th Street, the riders could plan tours through Yonkers to Tarrytown or to White Plains.

This wonderful train service was the forerunner of the popular New Haven, Jersey Central and Long Island bicycle trains of the 1930's.

THE NEW YORK BICYCLE EXPOSITION
Madison Square Garden, January 18-25, 1896

The New York Bicycle Exposition, January, 1896

Leslies' Weekly of January 30th, 1896 reports: "The bicycle show at the Madison Square Garden, which proved so attractive to the general public during the current week, is regarded by many as the best exhibition of the kind ever held in the country. The show was held under the auspices of the National Board of Trade and directed by President A. G. Spalding and Vice President R. Philip Gormully. A similar exhibit was held in Chicago, which also attracted thousands. Both shows were unprecedented successes both artistically and financially."

There were over 350 exhibits at the New York Show. The Fowler bicycle exhibit featured Sandow, the Tarzan of the era. It was reported that the ladies paid five cents for an opportunity to feel his flexed arm and shoulder muscles.

Today, these bicycle shows are still held by the trade but not open to the general public. They are usually held from January to March in Florida, New York, or elsewhere with thousands in attendance. The International Trade Shows manage this event.

Bicycle Police

During the bicycle boom of the 1890's, there was a need to establish law and order on the highways of America. Many communities organized bicycle police, whose duties included the apprehension of speeders, the prevention of cycle thievery and the checking of machines for legal equipment, such as bells and lamps. Some interesting problems were presented to the bicycle police.

According to *Bicycling World* of 1893. "Harry Glidden had a mania for stealing bicycles. He would note an unwatched machine, mount it and ride off, and then sell it. He was finally caught by the Salem, Massachusetts police as he was courting a well-known beauty of the city."

In 1894, editor "Merrie Wheeler" of the Women's Department, wrote under the heading of "Rowdy Rider," a complaint about both men and women cyclists. "They look untidy and delight in seeing how close they can get to running down a pedestrian or even a fellow cyclist."

Director Beitler in 1895, of the Philadelphia Police, established a detail of mounted police on cycles. They rigidly enforced the law requiring cycles to be equipped with bells and lamps. In Boston, the bicycle police were given orders, "to go out and get a few cyclists" for any infraction of bicycle ordinances.

Out in Little Rock, Arkansas, a Mrs. Noe was arrested by a cycle policeman for appearing in bloomers riding a

A SCORCHER FEELS THE STRONG ARM OF THE LAW 1890

SOME OF NEW YORK'S BICYCLE POLICEMEN

121

bicycle. When she was taken into court, Judge Wilson found for the defendant with this ruling: "Women have a constitutional and God given right to ride a bicycle and they are bound to wear comfortable and appropriate dress therefore."

The credit and honor of establishing the New York City bicycle police belongs solely to Police Commissioner Avery D. Andrews. He started the service on December 12th, 1895 with four patrolmen detailed for bicycle duty. This number was soon increased to 100 men. In 1896, the squad made 1,366 arrests of whom only 193 were discharged by the courts. This embraced everything from scorchers (fast riders who exceeded the legal speed limit of 8 miles an hour) to reckless riders. Another hazardous duty was to catch and stop run-away horses. The bicycle police were on duty from 10 a.m. to 5 p.m. and from 5 p.m. to midnight. Their uniforms were chosen for comfort, wear and appearance, comprising short tight fitting breeches, black stockings, and a buttoned jacket topped

PRIVATE STARKEY'S PRIVATE MISSION

Courtesy of *Steelways*-American Iron and Steel Industry

by a gray helmet. The men were armed with Colt 32's and night sticks and rode Wolff-American bicycles.

The *Bicycling World* also reported "The Story of an English Duke and an American Policeman." It tells of a young British nobleman arrested in Central Park in New York by a bicycle policeman for coasting (probably with his feet off the pedals, a dangerous practice as the rider has little control of the wheel). The reader was never told whether the duke was found guilty and fined.

By 1900, when autos were appearing on the highways, the speed laws were ammended to allow speeds from 15 to 35 miles an hour. However, during the 1935 cycling revival, I was apprehended again by the motor police of New York for pedalling with some club companions at the speed of about 15 miles an hour on Riverside Drive. All were given summonses to appear in traffic court for speeding. The traffic court clerk stated that the summons was ridiculous, but he sent the defendants to the felony court. The case was tried, all were charged with a violation and sentenced to a day in jail, or a fine of $2.00. All paid the fine, but it would have made an interesting news headline, "Bicyclists Fined for Speeding at 15 Miles an Hour, While Autos Pass By at 35 Miles an Hour Unchallenged."

Military Cycling

The uses of the bicycle in war time received serious consideration by our civilian and military leaders in the 1890's. A convention of Military Wheelmen was held in New York in 1895, and a proposal was made to establish a cycle infantry in the Army of the United States. The results of satisfactory tests of military cyclists covering long distances were presented to Generals Nelson A. Miles and Albert Ordway. The latter was the author of *Cycle Infantry Drill Regulations,* issued in 1892. Many of the state national guard units did organize cycle corps. Except for messenger services and reconoitering, the United States Army did not make use of the cycle infantry.

However, in 1898, a private named Starkey, a member of the United States Signal Corps, proved the capability of the bicycle for special service. In the Spanish-American War in Cuba, Starkey rode his bicycle ten miles to the rear of the Spanish forces and returned with vital military information unharmed, except for a tattered and torn uniform. Private Starkey made history as the first bicycle communicator in a shooting war!

European armies have regularly organized cycle regiments and corps and used them effectively. Emperor Alexander of Russia held the bicycle in high esteem. His cyclists "marched" 126 miles in 17 hours. In 1887, Lieutenant -Colonel A.R. Saville was made Commandant of the Cyclists' Corps of the British Army. He was Professor of Tactics of the Royal Military Academy at Sandhurst and originated many bicycle maneuvers. One year, France had 32,000 soldiers mounted on bicycles. A folding model, that weighed 29 pounds which could be collapsed and carried on the back of a soldier, was introduced in 1895. The German High Command allotted 100,000 marks to supply bicycles to their army. The Italians equipped their famous mountain troops with folding mini-type bicycles so popular today. Austria, Belgium, the Netherlands, Portugal and Switzerland all used military bicycles.

During World War I, fifty members of the Century Road Club Association of New York, including myself, volunteered to serve during the duration, in a cycling corps to General John Pershing. The Chiefs of Staff decided against the plan.

In World War II, the alert Japanese cycle infantry stormed and captured the once believed impregnable fortress at Singapore. The cyclists climbed over the fallen trees that would slow up military motor traffic like a swarm of ants on the attack.

In April of 1973, I was called to help organize a Cadet Cycling Club at the United States Military Academy at West Point. A meeting with cadet president Rheinhard Ratz was arranged to plan for cycling fun and fitness for the 120 eager cadets. Perhaps someday a cycling corps of cadets will stand at attention during dress parade alongside their mounts.

Many of our famous artists have portrayed the cycle infantry in action. Joseph Pennell has given us over 15 pictures of the corps and a long article, "Military Cycling" published in *The Graphic* for March 31st, 1888. Pennell has recently been elected to the American Bicycle Hall of Fame. Frederic Remington illustrated the story, "The Colonel of the First Cycle Infantry" in *Harper's Weekly* of May 18th, 1895. F. C. Yohn has pictured, "Bicycle Corps of an Infantry Regiment on Reconnaissance-Drill" of the 1895 period.

The present boom in cycling in America may again focus attention toward the use of the bicycle in war time.

HER SHOCKING ATTIRE
Drawn by F. M. Howarth

AMERICAN BICYCLE HALL OF FAME COMMITTEE
Photo by Al Hatos
Left to Right: Al Hatos, Roland Geist and James Paul

8
THE AMERICAN BICYCLE HALL OF FAME

THE AMERICAN BICYCLE HALL OF FAME, A national shrine to American bicycling was conceived at the 60th Annual Banquet of the Century Road Club Association of New York in 1959. Founder members included Captain Charles Staubach, Sylvin Segal, Lewis Heit, James C. Paul and myself.

The founders' aim was to establish non-profit educational museum under the Board of Regents of the State of New York. No officer or anyone connected with the Hall would be paid, and all work would be done on a volunteer basis.

President Loring McMillen of the Staten Island Historical Society offered us a large hall in the Richmond-

**THE NEW MOULTON STOWAWAY
FOLDING BICYCLE**
Designed by Alex Moulton of England 1970.
The model is on display in the Hall of Fame Museum
and was donated by HUFFY.

CUSTOM MADE UNICYCLES
The low model illustrated was donated by Roland
Geist and the high 32-foot model was donated
by Steven McPeak of Las Vegas, Nevada.
Both models are on display in the Hall
of Fame Museum.

town Historical Museum for our cycle collection, and
room in the library for our collection of bicycle books
and periodicals.

Donations arrived soon after the opening of the antique museum. Twenty-five old machines, ranging from
the 1869 boneshakers to the modern recumbent bicycle
called the "Futura," were donated. A motor-paced machine was given by Louis Maltese, Captain of the Century Road Club Association. Steven McPeak donated
(thru Bill Jenack of the Unicycling Society of America)
the 32-foot-high unicycle which he had ridden at Las
Vegas. Jim Paul donated the 1900 Columbia racer on
which he made the New York to Atlantic City record
about 1910. Al Hatos of the Century Road Club of
America donated some 100 old-time pictures of cycling
in New York. I donated my unicycle, as well as books
and jewelry. The Hall is lucky to have such a grand
group of sponsors. Hopefully, the old Frank Kramer
racing Pierce will be donated in the near future.

Once a year the Board of Governors meets on the third
Sunday of October to elect another member to the Hall
Roll of Fame. All riders are invited to participate in this
election by submitting names (along with reasons for the

choice) to the Board—comprised of James C. Paul,
James Maltese, Al Hatos and Secretary Roland C. Geist.
Nominations for the Hall Roll of Fame for 1978 are: Dr.
Allan Abbot, holder of the World Paced speed Record,
Steven McPeak, Nancy Baranet, Sue Novara and Sheila
Young.

On the same day, known as "Old Home Day," when the
Board of Governors meets, groups of cyclists ride down
from New York via South Ferry to participate in a show
of fancy riding by groups like The Wheelmen or the
Unicyclists. The Hall of Fame Museum is a public
museum open every day from 2 to 5 p.m. except on
Mondays. Visitors are invited to make a donation toward
the upkeep of the museum. Cash donations have been
received with thanks from Al Toefield of the United
States Cycling Federation and Louis Maltese of the
Century Road Club Association.

Plans have been drawn by an architect for a two-room
brick building. There will be a hall with pictures and
trophies of the great figures in the world of cycling. A
second room will be an old 1890 cycle shop with old
bicycles, tools, and machinery, a legacy from Mr. Rossbach, the New Brighton Bicycle Dealer of the 1880's.

126

BICYCLE EXHIBIT
Photo by Fungado
American Bicycle Hall of Fame Museum

THE FUTURA OF RECUMBENT BICYCLE
It was invented by Jack Fried of the Century Road
Club Association of New York in 1950. The original
model is on display at the Hall of Fame Museum.

The Working Committee

CURATOR—Loring McMillen, President of the Staten
Island Historical Society

SECRETARY—Roland C. Geist, Life Member Century
Road Club Association

MEMBER—Al Hatos, Century Road Club of America
Official Hall of Fame Pho-
tographer

MEMBER—Louis Maltese, Captain of the Century
Road Club Association,
Member of the United
States Cycling Federation

MEMBER—James C. Paul, Century Road Club Association and the League of
American Wheelmen

127

The American Bicycle
HALL OF FAME
1958

Margaret Gast - (1876-1968) Long distance women's champion in 1900. 2600 miles in 295 hours. Defeated the Champion of France.

Alfred Goullet - Won eight Six Day Races in the Madison Square Garden. One of America's Great Track Racers.

John Howard - Three times National Champion. Gold Medalist Pan American Games in 1971.

Adolph R. Jacobson - (1890-1950) Founder of the Amateur Bicycle League of America, Quarter Mile record holder in 1910.

Frank Kramer - (1880-1958) Holder of the Grand Prix de Paris 1905-06. World Sprint Champion 1912.

Dr. Paul B. Mac Cready - Inventor of the Gossamer Condor. First in history to make man-powered flight possible, August 23rd, 1977.

Audrey McElmury - First American woman to win the World Road championship in 1969. Holder of several national championships.

Charles M. Murphy - (1871-1950) Established the world's record in 1899 of a mile in 57.8 seconds in back of a Long Island Railroad train.

Joseph Pennell - (1860-1926) Honored bicycle artist, author and tourist awheel in America and Europe.

Albert A. Pope - (1843-1909) First American bicycle manufacturer, President Pope Manufacturing Company, Pioneer in the Good Roads Campaign.

Charles E. Pratt - (1845-1898) Founder and First President of the League of American Wheelmen. Author, poet and composer of songs.

Frank Small - (1896-1971) Founder member of the Amateur Bicycle League of America. Member of 1920 U.S.A. Olympic Track Team. Former editor of Bicycling magazine.

Monroe Smith - (1901-1972) Founder with wife Isabel of the American Youth Hostels, a 70,000-member organization of cyclists, hikers, and other outdoor sport enthusiasts.

Thomas Stevens - (1854-1935) First to pedal around the world alone on a high-wheel. Author of *Around the World on a Bicycle.*

Marshall (Major) Taylor - (1878-1932) Champion of the world in 1899. Author of *The Fastest Bicycle Rider in the World.* Greatest black cyclist of all time.

Dr. Paul Dudley White - (1886-1975) World famous cardiologist. Pioneer in the campaign to build safe cycling paths for America. Author of *Cycling in the School Fitness Program.*, Honorary president of The American Bicycle Hall of Fame for many years.

Arthur A. Zimmerman - (1869-1936) Champion of the World in 1893. Author of *Points for Cyclists with Training.* Considered the fastest sprinter of all time.

American Bicycle Hall of Fame Museum Collection
at the Richmondtown Restoration, Staten Island, New York

Antiques on Display
(Approximate Dates)

1869	Wooden Wheel Boneshaker Tricycle
1869	Boneshaker
1880	Ordinary Bicycle
1885	Star High-Wheel
1900	Chainless
1910	Touring Model
1920	English B.S.A. Fixed Gear Road Racer, James C. Paul of L.A.W.
1920	Columbia Road Racer with Fixed Gear, Sylvain Segal, C.R.C. Association
1930	Motor Paced Track Racer, Louis Maltese, C.R.C. Association
1940	Unicycle, low model, Roland C. Geist, C.R.C. Association
1960	High Unicycle 32 feet high, Steven McPeak of Las Vegas
1960	Futura, Recumbent Folding Model, Jack Fried - Inventor
1960	English Moulton Folding Model, Roland C. Geist and Huffy

Memorabilia in Show Cases
•Many shop items donated by Frank Rossbach, Staten Island, Bicycle Shop Dealer of 1880.
•Century Run Badges from some 35 New York Cycling Clubs - Segal and Geist.
•Twenty Championship Medals of the A.B.L.A. - Captain Louis Maltese.
•Twenty-five bicycle name plates from 1880 to 1900.
•Tray of bicycle jewelry, pins, spoons, and brooches - Roland C. Geist.
•Bells, repair kits, pumps, lamps, club banner - Frank Rossbach.

Hall Library
Secretary Roland C. Geist donated these books from his bicycle book library:

Baranet, Nancy Nieman, *Bicycling,* A.S. Barnes & Co., New York, 1973.
Bartleet, H.W., *Bartleet's Bicycle Book,* Ed. J. Burrow & Co. Ltd., London, 1931.
Geist, Roland C., *Bicycling as a Hobby,* Harper & Bros., New York, 1935.

Jacobs, Rene et al., *Velo 1977,* Private-Brussels, Belgium, 1977.
Lewis, Guy L. and Rodmond, Gerald, *Sporting Heritage - A Guide to American Halls of Fame,* A.S. Barnes, New Brunswick, 1974.
McWhirter, N. and Ross, *Guinness Book of World Records,* Bantam Books, Inc., New York, 1977.
Menke, Frank G., *The New Encyclopedia of Sports,* A.S. Barnes, New York, 1947.
Palmer, Arthur Judson, *Riding High,* E.P. Dutton & Co., New York, 1956.

Donated Magazines
American Bicyclist, Editor Stan. Gottlieb, New York.
Bicycle Journal, Editor Rix Quinn, Fort Worth, Texas.

THE COLUMBIA LIGHT ROADSTER—PRICE, $125
The original is on display in the Hall of Fame Museum

IS BICYCLING BAD FOR THE HEART?
By Charles Dana Gibson, 1897
Courtesy of Charles Scribners Sons

130

9
THE ART GALLERY

ART IN GENERAL HAS BEEN DEFINED AS any object, picture, or writing that brings enjoyment to the eyes and senses of the beholder.

The first part of this chapter will present the English hobby horse prints by such artists as Ackermann, Alken, Cruikshank, Heath, and Hudson. Thomas Tegg did much of the printing. The second part presents the modern artists of America, France, England and Mexico.

Most of the illustrations explain themselves. No amount of flowery language would enhance their value. As Picasso once said, "People who try to explain pictures are like dogs barking up the wrong tree."

The prints were selected on the basis of the fame of the artist, their historical importance, and their beauty and rarity.

The English Hobby Horse Artists

Rudolph Ackermann

Rudolf Ackermann was one of the outstanding English printmakers of the early eighteenth century. He was known as "the popularizer of aquatint engraving."

Ackermann (1764-1834) was born in Saxony. His father was a designer and builder of carriages, and had the honor of designing the funeral coach of Lord Nelson. Rudolph, however, was more interested in printmaking than carriages. In 1795, he moved to London and opened a print shop at 101 Strand. His shop soon became a rendezvous for of English art connoisseurs and remained so for a century. The introduction to his 1815 catalog reads, "R. Ackermann has fitted up a room of large dimensions, to receive an extensive collection of the most splendid publications, both ancient and modern. The Library is open for inspections daily and is brilliantly illuminated every evening with gas lights."

Several years later, he moved his books and prints to an ornate four-story building at 96 Strand. His 1830 catalog is designed to introduce "the Nobility and Gentry, the patrons of Art and People in general to his extensive stock in his new Repository of the Arts."

His most popular print of the 1819 period was "Johnson, the First Rider on the Pedestrian Hobby Horse." It is an accurate picture of the early top hatted rider and the

early machine. In the background are two racers traveling at all possible speed.

Henry Alken

Alken was born October 10, 1784 in Suffolk, England of Danish parentage. He worked as a stud groom to the Duke of Beaufort in his youth. Sports became his main interest. His father gave him his first drawing instruction; later he studied under John T. Beaumont.

In 1809 he married and began his career as a graphic journalist of sports. His drawings were taken from actual experiences; each print tells a story. Between 1792 and 1847 he exhibited 199 plates at the Royal Academy.

One biographer described him as a typical British sportsman, a downright good fellow whose virtues were loyalty, gaiety, generosity, justice and strength. Another writer states that Alken was afraid of criticism and self conscious toward visitors, stern with his children and an eccentric.

Facing page

JOHNSON, THE FIRST RIDER ON THE PEDESTRIAN HOBBY HORSE
By Rudolph Ackermann

Above

JOHNSON'S PEDESTRIAN HOBBY HORSE RIDING SCHOOL
By Henry Alken, 1819
Courtesy of the U.S. National Museum, Washington, D.C.

His most famous bicycle print was "Johnson's Pedestrian Hobby Horse Riding School." It was printed by Ackermann in 1819. (I purchased the picture in London some thirty years ago for $25.) It now decorates my study along with the rare Currier and Ives velocipede print.

In his later days the artist took to wearing old-fashioned attire, and was an odd sight on the streets of London. He died of a tumor on April 7, 1851.

After his death it was said, "Prints, sketches oils, pictures and lively water colors were the legacy he bequested to his country and in such large numbers, it is impossible to say how many."

George Cruikshank

Cruikshank was the most prolific of the English caricaturists of the hobby horse fad. He derived his artistry from Hogarth and his style from Gillray. The artist lived in an age of extravagance and poverty. It was said that he had the habit of scratching the interesting faces he noted on the streets upon his thumbnails.

Among his better known prints are the two illustrated. "Every Man on His Perch or Going to the Hobby Fair" presents almost every known profession and trade of the period. "The (Hobby) Horse Dealer" presents horse trading. A buyer says "I can see he has been down once or twice." The dealer answers, "I'll warrant him sound sir and free from Vice." The three horses looking on from their stable take a very apprehensive view of the proceedings.

At the age of 84 he still danced the hornpipe. Cruikshank died in his London home on February 1, 1878. His body rests in St. Paul's Church.

A modern artist has characterized him as follows: "Nearly every etched illustration by Cruikshank is a carefully studied picture, every part is related to the intended effect of the whole." He is remembered as one of the greatest comic artists who ever lived.

134

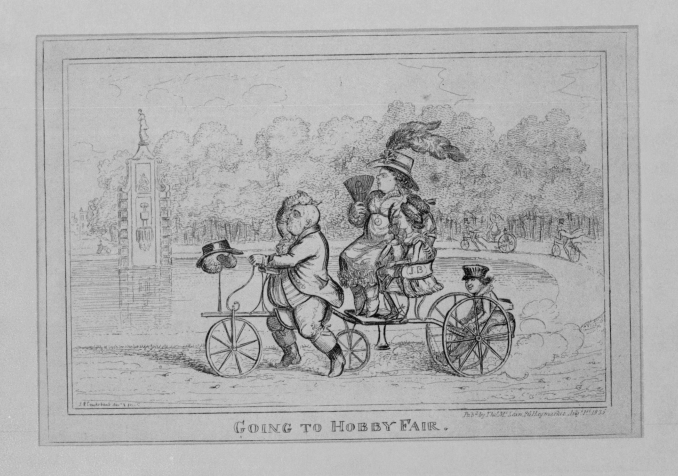

GOING TO HOBBY FAIR.

Facing page
THE (HOBBY) HORSE DEALER
By George Cruikshank and Humphrey

Above
GOING TO HOBBY FAIR
By George Cruikshank

William Heath

Heath was an English artist and engraver. He was born in 1795 and died at Hampstead in 1840. His artistry included water color and copper plate engravings. Heath specialized in humorous and historic subjects. Many of his prints are on exhibit in the printroom of the British Museum in London.

"Modern Pegasus or Dandy Hobbies in Full Speed," was printed by T. Tegg. It shows a hobby horse race about 1819 with a heavyweight rider leading the thin man in a sprint finish that raises the highway dust.

J. Hudson

This English engraver of the 1819 era has produced a most interesting portrait of a highway accident, in his "An Unexpected Occurrence."

A bull has charged a horseman and the hobby horse riders are also in trouble; one has fallen into the water

MODERN PEGASUS or *Dandy Hobbies in full Speed*

and his machine is wrecked, while the other rider has lost control of his hobby horse.

T.Tegg

Most of the hobby horse print caricatures illustrated in this book were drawn by Thomas Tegg of London.

Tegg, the son of a grocer, was born at Wimbledon in Surrey, now the famous tennis center of England, on March 4, 1776. He became an orphan at the age of five and at nine was a bound apprentice to a publisher. The youth was treated badly and soon ran away to wander through Ireland and Wales.

On his return to England, he served with John and Arthur Arch, Quaker booksellers of London. His interest in the book and print business increased and became his life career. On April 20, 1800, he married and opened a book shop with a partner Dewick. The business lost money through the treachery of a friend. Tegg then obtained a country auction license and became a successful auctioneer. He returned to London in 1805 and opened a shop at 111 Cheapside, which was an instant success. Here he printed pamphlets and pictures. By 1840 he had published over 4,000 books, of which less than twenty were failures.

In 1824, he opened up a larger shop at 73 Cheapside. This versatile book and printmaker, seller and auctioneer died April 21, 1845 and was buried at Wimbledon.

(I am indebted to Research Assistant Mrs. Dinah Southern of the Department of Prints and Drawings of The British Museum in London, for the biography of T. Tegg.)

The print entitled "Anti-Dandy Infantry" was made when hobby horse riders were in disfavor in English villages. It portrays a rider being roughly treated by a local merchant; the blacksmith who is breaking the hobby horse.

136

Facing page

**MODERN PEGASUS OR DANDY HOBBIES
IN FULL SPEED**
By William Heath and Thomas Tegg

Above

AN UNEXPECTED OCCURRENCE
By J. Hudson

Top
A FAMILY PARTY TAKING AN AIRING
By Thomas Tegg, 1819

Bottom
GOING TO THE RACES
By Thomas Tegg, 1819

138

Top

**THE NEW LONG BACK'D HOBBY MADE
TO CARRY THREE WITHOUT KICKING**
By Thomas Tegg

Bottom

ANTI-DANDY INFANTRY
By Thomas Tegg

Above

MILITARY HOBBY HORSES
Unsigned

Facing page:
Top

**LES ANCÊTRES DE LA BICYCLETTE
(LES CÉLÉRIFÈRES) SOUS
LE DIRECTORIE**

Bottom

A ROYAL HOBBY
Unsigned

Currier and Ives

Nathaniel Currier was born in Roxbury, Massachusetts in 1813. He moved to New York and opened an art shop with a partner, though the partnership was soon dissolved. He then moved to Wall Street, New York. Here he made prints of steamships, railroads, and country life.

James Merritt Ives was employed as a bookkeeper for Mr. Currier. He became interested in the prints, and wound up in a partnership with Currier.

Their lithographs sold well and their shop held all the excitement of a newspaper office. The small folio prints sold from 15 cents to 25 cents and the large prints from $1.50 to $3. Their "Darktown Comics" sold over 73,000 copies. The skating scene in Central Park, New York, recently sold for over $1,000.

Mr. Currier retired in 1880 and died in 1888. Mr. Ives carried on the business until his death in 1895. Unfortunately, the young Currier and Ives did not inherit their parents' gift. In 1907, the firm passed out of existence.

Today, their prints are in great demand. A Mr. Peters, a Currier and Ives art collector, amassed over 5,735 prints now donated to the Library of Congress, the Museum of the City of New York, and a California library.

The print illustrated, "The Velocipede," is explained by the artists: "We can beat the swiftest steed, with our new Velocipede."

It was produced in 1869 and the last price at an auction sale was $300. I bought it at "The Old Print Shop" in New York fifty years ago at $50. It is a rare picture.

Thomas Worth

Worth was born in New York City in 1834 and died in 1917. He lived in both Long Island and Staten Island.

He was both a comic and genre artist. Some of Dicken's books were illustrated by him. In 1855 Worth

sold prints to Nathaniel Currier, and later worked as a lithographer for Currier and Ives.

The print entitled, *"The Velocipede Mania - What It May Come To"* was published in *Harper's Weekly* in 1869. The characters are well drawn. Notice the gentleman in his top hat leaving the riding school with his arm in a sling!

Frederick Burr Opper

Opper was born in 1857 and was one of America's great cartoonists.

In his early years, Opper was associated with Keppler and together they produced most of the comics for *Puck*.

Author William Allen Rogers wrote, "He (Opper) has made more people laugh than any one else in the country."

Opper died in 1937.

Facing page

THE VÉLOCIPÈDE
By Currier and Ives, 1869
"We can beat the swiftest steed,
With our new velocipede."

Above

**THE VÉLOCIPÈDE MANIA—
WHAT IT MAY COME TO!**
By Thomas Worth

Top
A TOUR OF THE PICKWICK CYCLING CLUB IN FRANCE
By Joseph Pennell

Bottom
THE WAGGON AND HORSES, BECKHAMPTON
By Frank Patterson
From Dicken's "Bagman's Story"

144

Joseph Pennell and Elizabeth Robbins Pennell

Of all the artists who portrayed bicycling, the most unique were the Pennells. They toured thousands of miles around Europe on their tandem tricycle and bicycles and wrote and illustrated their adventures in many volumes.

Joseph Pennell was born in Philadelphia in 1860 and studied at the Pennsylvania Academy of Fine Arts in Philadelphia. He won many awards and exhibited in the United States, Paris, Dresden, Milan, and Amsterdam. The New York Public Library lists over a 100 of his prints. In 1951, he received a postumous award of an Honorary Degree of Doctor of Laws from the University of Pennsylvania.

Some of his cycling experiences are recorded in: *"A Canterbury Pilgrimage"* in 1885, *"An Italian Pilgrimage"* in 1887, *"France and Italy"* in 1893, *"Over the Alps on a Bicycle"* in 1898, *"Two Pilgrims Progress"* in 1899. Most of these volumes were written with his wife as co-author and co-rider.

Their biographer, Edward L. Tinker, reports interesting stories of their cycling tours. One day, they covered 108 miles; one summer, they crossed ten of the highest Alpine passes within six weeks on their bicycles. Mrs. Pennell was always ready to ride although she once complained it was a relief when they finally exchanged their tandem for separate bicycles. (The long wheelbase makes uphill tandem riding very laborious, in my own experience of over 10,000 miles on a tandem.)

Joseph Pennell died in 1926. The Pennells left a rich heritage to the cycling world. My collection includes 10 Pennell sketches.

The illustration "A Tour of the Pickwick Cycling Club in France" shows members of England's first bicycle touring club, around 1885, riding the tandem tricycle, high wheels and safeties. The Club president was usually known by the assumed name of Mr. Pickwick.

Frank Patterson

For over 50 years "Pat", as he was affectionately called, devoted himself to sketching bicycle touring in England. He was born in 1871 and submitted his first bicycle sketch in 1893. He produced over 5,000 sketches to the *Cycling* magazine of London. Two volumes have been published of his best work.

His drawings were unique in their use of white space. The bicycles were always mechanically correct and the settings were always picturesque. "The Waggon and Horses" presents a typical English tourist awheel stopping off at the inn for his long awaited cup of tea.

In 1944, he won the Bidlake Memorial Prize for his "joyous delineation of cycling." "Pat" gave the longest service of any newspaper illustrator in England.

Editor H. H. England wrote of "Pat" in 1952, "Patterson is dead, but "Pat's" interpretation of bicycle touring will live forever."

Honoré Daumier

Daumier is one of the great French satirical graphic artists. He lived between 1808 and 1879.

At the age of 14 he wanted to draw and soon attended art school. In 1832, he was sent to prison for six months for his caricature of Louis Philipe. He drew hundreds of street scenes and loved to make caricatures of people, especially those in the legal profession. His satire is profoundly human. For many years he drew pictures for the periodical *"La Caricature."*

The illustration "Mon Velocipede" shows "Peace" astride a canon. I bought this rare print, in Paris, while on a European cycling tour.

Charles Dana Gibson

This famous artist was born in Roxbury, Massachusetts in 1867, and soon showed a talent for art. Gibson was a leading illustrator for *Life* magazine at a salary of $250 a month, which was very high in those days.

He was best known for his pen and ink sketches of American womanhood, known as the "Gibson Girl." He also portrayed the socially prominent men and women of America. His inspired drawings were said to have touched the hearts and enriched the minds of thousands of people.

His clever sketch entitled "Is Bicycling Bad for the Heart?" was drawn at a time when the medical profession of America was considering the dangers of bicycling for women. He also produced many sketches of such popular sports as swimming, football, golf and tennis.

Gibson died in 1944, leaving a rich heritage of Americana of the Gay Nineties.

Harrison Fisher

This artist was born in Brooklyn on July 17, 1875. He studied in San Francisco but lived and worked in New York. His illustrations were published in the *Saturday Evening Post*, *Scribners* and *McClures* as well as in many books of the 1890 period. He was best known for his sketches of the American girl.

The pen and ink drawing illustrated was photographed from an original which I bought from a New York art dealer about 1930. It is an excellent example of the artist's work. The costumes of both man and woman are correct as I remember the era.

Harrison Fisher died in 1934.

WHEELING ALONG TOGETHER
By Harrison Fisher

MON VÉLOCIPÈDE
By Honoré Daumier

Frederic Remington

This famous American painter, sculptor and illustrator was born in Canton, New York in 1861. He studied at the Yale Art School. Because he lived for many years as a cowboy, hunter and farmer in the west, his subjects were often drawn from plains life. He illustrated for *Collier's* and *Harper's* magazines.

The Remington pictures were exhibited at the Metropolitan Museum of Art in New York, the National Gallery and the Corcoran Gallery in Washington. In 1961, a commemorative postage stamp was issued in his honor. He died in 1909.

Illustrated is his "The Tortoise and the Hare." The poem explains the print:

"Oh Life, you're sure a tortoise,
And Science you're a hare
Yet, if I can have the tortoise
For Science I'll not care -
He passed us by at the top of the grade,
But we all picked him up at the bottom of the grade,
We picked up the pieces and we sat 'em in the shade,
With a punctured tire and a split shoulder blade
And if I can keep the tortoise
The world can keep the hare!"

THE TORTOISE AND THE HARE
By Frederic Remington

148

Toulouse-Lautrec

Toulouse-Lautrec is a great name in the world of art. He was born in Albi, France on November 24, 1864. Paris was his studio. As a youth, he injured his thigh, and was crippled for life. Unable to ride a bicycle, he became an ardent race fan and was a well known habitue of the Velodrome Buffalo in Paris. He found the professional bicycle racers of great interest.

At the Velodrome, he met and saw the great American world champion Zimmerman. Illustrated is the quick sketch he produced.

Toulouse-Lautrec's art has been summed up by his contemporaries: "He towered above all other sketch and poster artists in artistic but not in physical stature." Being a heavy drinker he suffered a stroke at the age of 37 in 1901. He was a man of dignity, charm, generousity, wit and gaiety.

Jose Guadalupe Posada

This great Mexican artist ranks with the European bicycle artists. He was born in Aguascalientes, Mexico on February 2, 1852. His parents were of peasant stock. He worked in the fields and in a pottery factory in his youth. He soon showed a talent for art.

About 1887, he moved to Mexico City and set up an art shop. Previously, he had worked with a lithographer in Leon. This had given him experience in etching and wood block engraving. In the next twenty years, he had produced over 20,000 engravings. His prints were published on cheap quality paper and were sold on newsstands, cafes and on the streets.

Illustrated is his popular print "The Cycling Skeletons," in which a group of skeletons cycle on after death.

Posada is considered the outstanding popular folk artist of Mexico. Orozco, another great Mexican artist, writes, "Posada is the equal of the greatest artists in simplicity, humility, equilibrium and dignity." He influenced the work of both Orozco and Riviera.

He died in poverty in Mexico City on January 20, 1913.

Salvador Dali

Salvador Domenech Felipe Jacinto Dali was born near Barcelona, Spain on May 11, 1904. His father was interested in both art and folk dancing. Salvador began his artistic career at an early age by scratching pictures on his table with a fork. When older, he attended art school and painted during his summer vacations. In 1916, he stated, "I am an Impressionist." While attending the School of Fine Arts in Madrid, he was involved in an uprising and spent a month in jail.

In 1925, he exhibited his work in Barcelona and in 1928 established himself in Paris. There he met Gala, his wife, and they soon bought a small home in a Spanish fishing village at Port Lligat. Back in Paris they enjoyed the social life, and visited the United States several times.

Many people believe Dali is an eccentric; he reportedly tossed a bathtub through a show window, and once gave a public lecture wearing a diving suit. However, Dali is also considered one of the world's greatest surrealist painters.

The bicycle portrait entitled "Sentimental Colloquy" was completed in 1944. Dali delightfully blended references to two art forms, music and cycling. The original masterpiece is in the collection of Mr. and Mrs. A. Reynolds Morse of the Salvador Dali Museum at Beach Wood, Cleveland, Ohio. The museum is operated as an educational project and may be visited by appointment.

Fernand Leger

Fernand Leger was born in Normany in 1881. He attended the Ecole des Beaux Artes in Paris.

He became one of France's outstanding painters. His works won many prizes and were exhibited in Paris, New York, Philadelphia, Chicago and San Francisco. He conducted an art school in both Paris and New York and his paintings were very popular. He was widely known as one of the leaders of the cubist school.

Leger produced twelve bicycle prints, including "Big Julie" which is typical of the cubist school. "Big Julie" depicts a muscular woman cyclist together with a flower, a butterfly and aspects of a bicycle.

Pablo Picasso

This great Spanish painter, sculptor, graphic artist and ceramist was born in Malaga in 1881. He was a precocious youth and was admitted at 15 to the advanced class at the Royal Academy of Art at Barcelona. His art is exhibited in most of the great art galleries of the world. His favorite subjects were women, musical instruments, bulls and other animals.

In 1943, he made a bronze cast of parts of a bicycle; the saddle and handlebar resembled a bull's head. There was much confusion as to whether the painting was really art. Picasso said, "You know, today I saw a bicycle seat and a handle bar that looked like a bull's head to me." Picasso imagined he recognized a bull's head and went on to create a masterpiece.

This master of modern art died on April 9, 1973. "Goat Skull and Bottle", 1951, is another imaginative treatment of the bicycle motif. A whimsical collection of items includes handlebars used as goat's horns and bicycle spokes as flower petals.

ZIMMERMAN
By Toulouse-Lautrec
Courtesy of the Prints Division, New York Public Library; Astor, Lenox, and Tilden Foundation

THE CYCLING SKELETONS
By Jose Guadalupe Posada

Courtesy of the Metropolitan Museum of Art;
Gift of Joan Charlet 1930

SENTIMENTAL COLLOQUY
By Salavado Dali, 1944

Courtesy of Mr. and Mrs. A. Reynolds Morse, Salvador Dali Museum,
Cleveland (Beachwood) Ohio

BIG JULIE
By Fernand Leger

Courtesy of the Museum of Modern Art, New York;
Lillie P. Bliss Bequest

GOAT, SKULL AND BOTTLE
By Pablo Picasso, 1951
Bicycle parts are used in the work
Courtesy of the Museum of Modern Art,
the Mrs. Simon Guggenheim Fund

155

FAST GETAWAY
By Norman Rockwell
Courtesy of Roland Geist

156

Norman Rockwell

America's most beloved illustrator was born in New York City on February 3, 1894 and died on November 9, 1978. At the age of 14 he left high school and was accepted as a student at the Art Student's League. At 18, a full-time professional artist, he made his first cover for *The Saturday Evening Post,* May 20, 1916. Since then he has produced 317 covers for this popular magazine. At 19 he became art illustrator for *Boy's Life.*

In 1943 Rockwell's studio at Arlington, Vermont, was burned to the ground and many of his finest creations were destroyed; only the family bicycles were rescued. His studio is now located at Stockbridge, Massachusetts. His sons have been his models for many scouting illustrations.

Illustrated in this book is a reproduction of an original painting I purchased some 40 years ago. It shows the schoolboys happily leaving school, and was entitled *Fast Getaway.* Rockwell has the rare ability to portray the everyday lives of Americans. A grand collection of his magazine covers may be seen at *The Saturday Evening Post* Museum in Independence Square, Philadelphia.

He resided in the Berkshire Hills where he would pedal his favorite bicycle with Mrs. Rockwell.

Norman Rockwell was elected to the American Bicycle Hall of Fame in New York City. His picture is exhibited alongside that of the earlier great cyclist artist Joseph Pennell.

Bicycle Art Reference Books

Furstenau, Oscar, *Radlerei,* Graphische Institute, Leipzig c. 1895.

Patterson, Frank, *The Patterson Book,* Temple Press, London, 1948.

Patterson, Frank, *The Second Patterson Book,* Edited by H. H. England Temple Press, London, 1952.

Saunier, Dollfus and Geoffrey, *Histoire de la Locomotion Terrestre,* L'Illustration, Paris, 1936.

Simm, Franz, *Skizzen aus der Radler Sport,* Franz Hanfstangel, Munich, c. 1895.

Sport Album, *Rad Welt,* Strauss, Berlin, 1913 (pictures of the world champions).

Streamer, Volney, *The World Awheel,* Frederick A. Stokes and Co., New York, 1896.

APPENDICES

Appendix A

LISTING OF ORGANIZATIONS WITH RELATED CYCLING ACTIVITIES

American Rail Bike Association, P.O. Box 9952, Colorado Springs, Colorado 80932.

Bicycle Airplane Flyers - The International Human Powered Vehicle Association, California State University, Long Beach, California 90840.

Southern Veteran - Cycle Club, 198 Sherwood Park Road, Micham, Surrey CR 4 INF England.

The Wheelmen, 335 S. Waverly, Dearborn, Michigan 48124.

Unicycling Society of America, 67 Lion Lane Westbury, Long Island, New York 11590.

United States Bicycle Polo Association, P.O. Box 565 FDR Station, N.Y. 10022.

Appendix B

CLASSIFIED BICYCLE BIBLIOGRAPHY

Compiled from the card catalogs of the New York Public Library (Main Branch) and the Library of Congress at Washington D.C.

Topical

Touring	135 Volumes
General	102
Racing, Training and Health	49
Fiction	48
History	35
Guides	34
Technical	27
Autobiography and Biography	23
Cycling Clubs and Stories	17
Patent Records	12
Poetry and Songs	12
Women Cycling	5
Bicycle Art	3

Languages

English	341
French	66
German	41
Italian	11
Russian	9
Japanese	6
Spanish	6
Others	22

Appendix C

Selected Bibliography of Older, Generally Out-Of-Print Bicycling Books
1869 -1940

(Many may be obtained from the Library of Congress)

Abridgements of Specifications - Velocipedes, Her Majesty's Stationery Office, London 1877 to 1908.
Allen, J.T., *Digest of Cycles or Velocipedes - United States Patents 1789 to 1898,* New York Engraving and Printing Co., Washington D.C.
Bartleet, H.W., *Bartleet's Bicycle Book,* (The Coventry Collection) E.J. Burrow, London, 1931.
Bottomley, J.F.B., *The Velocipede,* Simpkin, Marshall and Co., London, 1869.
Dark Blue Bicycle Club - *Bicycling Captain Crawley Handbook,* Ward Lock and Co. London, 1878.
Duncan, H.O., *Vinctans de Cyclisme Practique,* F. Juren, Paris, 1897.
Goddard, J.T., *The Velocipede,* Hurd and Houghton, New York, 1869.
Griffin, Harry Hewitt, *Bicycles and Tricycles of 1879,* The Bazaar, London, 1879.
Hoffman, Professor, *Tips for Tricyclists,* Frederick Warne and Co., London, 1887.
Jupitor (Rovers Bicycle Club), *Velocipedia,* (A Bicycling Burlesque Extravaganza), T.G. Weston, London, 1880.
Practical Bicyclist, *The Bicycle,* Ward Lock and Company, London, 1880.
Pratt, Charles E., *The American Bicycler,* Houghton Osgood and Co., Boston, 1879.
Saunier, Dollfus, Geoffrey, *Histoire de la Locomotion Terrestre,* (Volture, Cyclisme, Auto), L'Illustration, Paris, 1936.
Spencer, Charles, *The Bicycle, Its Use and Action,* Frederick Warne and Co., London, 1870.
Spencer, Charles, *The Modern Bicycle,* Frederick Warne and Co., London, 1876.
Sturmey, Henry, *The Complete Guide to Bicycling,* Iliffe and Sons, Coventry, 1882.
Sturmey, Henry, *Tip Top Tales - Bicycle Ben or The Lion of Lightening Lode,* Aldine Publishing Co., London, c 1880.
Velox Velocipedes, *Bicycles and Tricycles,* George Routledge & Sons, London, 1869.

Appendix D

Bicycle Periodicals

For The Industry:

    American Bicyclist, Editor Stan Gottlieb, Cycling Press, 461, 8th Avenue, New York, N.Y. 10001.

    The Bicycle Journal, Editor Rix Quinn, Quinn Publications, P.O. Box 1570, Fort Worth, Texas 76101.

For The Cyclist:

    League of American Wheelmen Bulletin, Editor Phyllis Harmon, 19 South Bothwell, Palatine, Illinois 60067.

    Bicycle Forum, Editor Dan Burden, P.O. Box 68, Silver Spring, Maryland 20907.

    Bicycling, 33 Minor Street, Emmaus, Pennsylvania, 18049.

    Bike World, Box 2681, Boulder, Colorado 80322.

    Boom in Bikeways, Editor James J. Hayes, Bicycle Manufacturers Association, 1101 15 Street N.W., Washington D.C. 20005.

    Competition Cycling, Editor Jim McFadden, P.O. Box 2066, Carson City, Nevada 89701.

    Cycle Touring, Editor H. John Way, Cyclists Touring Club, 69 Meadrow, Godalming, Surrey, England GU7-3HS.

    The Boneshaker, Editor Derek Roberts, 198 Sherwood Park Road, Mitcham, Surrey, England CR4 1-NF.

    The Wheelmen, Editor G. Donald Adams, 335 South Waverly, Dearborn, Michigan 48124.

    Velo News, Editor Ed Pavelka, Box 1257, Brattleboro, Vermont 05301.

Appendix E

Libraries and Museums

*Whose staffs have kindly offered information
in the preparation of this book*

United States

American Bicycle Hall of Fame	New York, N.Y.
Salvador Dali Museum	Cleveland, Ohio
Donnell Art Library	New York, N.Y.
Library of Congress	Washington, D.C.
Library and Museum of the Performing Arts Lincoln Center	New York, N.Y.
Metropolitan Museum of Art	New York, N.Y.
Museum of the City of New York	New York, N.Y.
Museum of Modern Art	New York, N.Y.
New York Historical Society	New York, N.Y.
New York Public Library, Main Branch	New York, N.Y.
Pennsylvania Academy of Fine Arts	Philadelphia, Pa.
Philadelphia Museum of Art	Philadelphia, Pa.
Smithsonian Institution	Washington, D.C.

Austria

Technisches Museum Fur Industrie und Gewerbe	Vienna

England

British Museum Library	London
Herbert Art Gallery and Museum	Coventry
Science Museum	London

France

Musee National de la Voiture	Compiegne
Musee Conservatoire National des Arts et Metiers	Paris

Germany

Deutsches Museum	Munich

Japan

Museum of Transportation	Tokyo

Appendix F

International Organizations

United States
Touring

American Youth Hostels	Delaplane, Virginia 22025.
League of American Wheelmen	19 South Bothwell, Palatine Illinois 60067.
The Wheelmen	335 South Waverly, Dearborn Michigan, 48124.

International Bicycle Touring Society	846 Prospect Street,
	La Jolla, California 92037.
	Racing
United States Cycling Federation Inc.	101 Maiden Lane,
	New York, N.Y.

England

Touring

Cyclists Touring Club	Cotterell House,
	69 Meadrow, Godalming
	Surrey, England GU7-3HS.
Southern Veteran Cycle Club	198 Sherwood Park Road,
	Micham, Surrey, England
	CR 4-INF.

Appendix G

American Bicycle Manufacturers

The Bicycle Manufacturers Association of America Inc., 1101 15th Street, NW, Washington D.C. 20005.
AMF Wheel Goods Division, P.O. Box 344, Olney, Illinois 62450.
Chain Bike Corporation, 350 Beach 79 Street, Rockaway Beach, New York, N.Y. 11693.
Columbia Manufacturing Company, Westfield, Massachusetts 01085.
Huffy Corporation, Dayton, Ohio 45401.
Murray Ohio Manufacturing Company, Brentwood, Tennessee 37027.
Schwinn Bicycle Company, 1856 North Kostner Avenue, Chicago, Illinois 60639.

Appendix H

The Early Bicycle Songs

My song collection, numbering 152, was started about 1925. Only 135 are listed here because many are in foreign languages.
Mr. W.N.H. Harding, a musicologist from Chicago, has kindly supplied information on the early songs included.

Year	Title	Composer	Publisher
1869	The Flying Velocipede	Brio	Wm. A. Pond, New York
	The Gay Velocipede	Cooper and Miller	J.L. Peters, New York
	The Great Velocipede song from Sinbad		W.A. Pond, New York
	the Sailor		
	The New Velocipede	E.H. Sherwood	J.P. Shaw, Rochester, New York
	the Unlucky Velocipedist	S. Low Coach	Blackman, New Orleans

162

Year	Title	Author/Composer	Publisher
	The Velocipede Set	E. Mack	Lee and Walker, Philadelphia
	Velocipede	Chas. Koppitz	Koppitz, Prufer and Co., Boston
	Velocipede (Galop)	M.F.H. Smith	C.C. Sawyer, Brooklyn
	The Velocipede	William Jay	William E. Millet and Son, New York
	Velocipede Galop	Harry B. Hart	C.H. Ditson Co., New York
	Velocipedia	Frank Howard and Horace Kimball	Root and Cady, Chicago
	Velocipediana	A.L. Adamas	Wm. A. Pond, New York
	Velocipede Johnny		H. DeMarsan, New York
	Velocipede	William A. Fiske	S. Brainard and Sons, Cleveland
	Velocipede Song		Wm. A. Pond, New York
1880	Bicycle Glide	W. Diederich	Lee and Walker, Philadelphia
1882	Star Bicycle Galop	Chas. W. Nathan	Spear and Denhoff, New York
	Bicycle March	N.R. Graham	J.L. Brodersen, Chicago
1883	Bicycle Galop	William H. Hall	R.A. Spalding, Troy
	Bicycle Galop	Mollenhaupt	S. Brainards & Sons, Cleveland
	The Star Rider	John Ford	H.B. Smith Machine Co., Smithville N.J.
	The Wheelman's Song	John Ford	H.B. Hart, Philadelphia
1884	The Song of the Wheel	Chas. E. Pratt	The Wheelman Co., Boston
	The Wheelman's Song	William J. Stabler	Outing, Boston
1885	Bicycle Waltz	J.J. Sawyer and Geo. E. Jackson	W.A. Evans, Boston
1886	The League Waltz	George Fred Brooks	Edward Schuberth Co., New York
	Its Best to Keep Up With the Style	H.G. Wheeler and J.W. Wheeler	Shaw, New York
1887	Bicycle Galop	Ludwig Andre	William Rohlfing and Co., Milwaukee
	Swiftly and Silently	J.J. Chickering and H.T. Smith	Ellis, Washington D.C.
	Wheel on to Glory	Hubbard T. Smith	John F. Ellis and Co., Washington, D.C.
1888	The Wheelmans Song	Dunnelly and Speck	T.B. Harmes, New York
1890	Cycle Polka	Geo W. Wallace	Wm. A. Pond, New York
1891	The Maid of Ixion and The Cycle Man	James Meakins	Meakins, New York
1892	Daisy Bell	Harry Dacre	T.B. Harmes, New York
	Bicycle March	Laurent L. Combs	White Smith and Co., Boston
1893	March Bicyclysto	Eugene Angel	Ilsen and Co., Cincinnati
	Since Katie Rides a Wheel	C. Harris and Clauder	Harris, Milwaukee
	Wheeling Away to Glory	W.W. Wave	Wm. Delaney, New York
1894	Arthur Dear or Daisy Bell's Reply	J. Austin Springer	Capital, Albany
	The Bloomers	Schrage and Potstock	Wm. Potstock Co., Chicago
	Carrie and Her Wheel	Theo H. Northrup	Treloer Music Co., Mexico, Mo.
	Hurrah for the Girls in Bloomers	Arnold Somlyo	S. Brainards Sons, Chicago
	Merry Cycle Song	Roland Hennessy	Witmark and Sons, New York
	Mulrooney on a Bike	Emmet Duffy	C.H. Kimball, Manchester N. Hampshire
	The Scorcher	Eugene Kramer	Edward A. Saalfeld, Chicago
1895	Angel Grace and the Crimson Rim	Post and Edwards	Robt. De Young, St. Louis
	Arrow Cycling Club Two Step	Joe Mahany	Anthony Kiefer, Peoria, Ill.
	The Belle of the Wheel	Julius V. Bernauer	Bureau of Literature, Chicago
	The Bicycle Girl	A Bicycle Boy	J.B. Millet Co., Boston
	The Bicycle Girl	Oddfellow and Meacham	Hedenberg and Dakin, Brooklyn
	Bloomer Two Step March	M. Florence	T.B. Harms, New York
	Climbing on My Golden Wheel	Harry J. Ballou	Oliver Ditson, Boston
	Courting on a Wheel	Ed Rogers	M. Witmark and Sons, New York

	Title	Composer	Publisher
	The Cycling Maid or	Grant and Southwide	National, Chicago
	The Bicycles the Thing		
	Doolin and His Bike	Lawlror and Blake	Crescent Publishing Co., New York
	Excelsior March	Edward E. Rice	T.B. Harms, New York
	Get Your Lamps Lit	Theo. A. Metz	Theo A. Metz, New York
	He's Got Wheels in His Head	Charles Robinson	Howley Haviland New York
1895	Have You a Wheel?	O.A. Hoffman	Hoffman Publishing Co., Milwaukee
	Johannah, Is Your Heart Still True?	George Evans	S. Brainards Sons, Chicago
	Keating Galop	G.H.R. Miller	Phelps Music Co. New York
	Keating Wheel March	Ray Woodman Bryan	Keating Wheel, Holyoke
	Love on Wheels	M. Stuart and Percy Gaunt	Hamilton Gordon, New York
	Mary Belle	W.M. Joseph	Ditson and Co., Boston
		and Louis Mac Evoy	
	Ridin' on de Golden Bike	Dave Reed Jr.	M. Witmark and Sons, New York
	Since Hannah Done Learned	G.L. Davis	Hitchcock, New York
	to Ride a Wheel		
	The United States Wheel March	Chas. Smith Tarbox	Chicago Stamping, Chicago
	Wheeling, Wheeling or	Danzig and Banta	H. Haviland, New York
	Love on Wheels		
	Wheelmen's Patrol	Frank P. Banta	Howley, Haviland and Co., New York
1896	Ben Hur March	Bell and Cody	Central Cycle Mfg Co., Indianapolis
	The Bicycle Girl	F.S. Howe	J.E. Ditson and Co., Philadelphia
	Brooklyn Bicycle Club March	W.J. Mc Intyre	G.A. Kornder, Brooklyn
	Century Run	Chas. D. Blake	Oliver Ditson Co., Boston
	The Cyclist March	R.E. Wagner	Cundy Music Co., Boston
	The Cycle Queen	T.P. Brooke	John Church Co., Cincinnati
	The Cycle King	Al.F. Kuhn	The John Church Co., New York
	The Dayton March	W.H. Thomas	F.L. Barnard, Lynn, Mass.
	Give Me the Girls That Ride a Wheel	Donoghue	Schaller
	The Gody Wheeling Glee	Coverly and Hughes	Gody Magazine, New York
	Julienne	Dave Reed Jr.	M. Witmark and Sons, New York
	L.A.W. March	W.H. Hosmer	Ford and Styles, Lynn, Mass.
	L.A.W. Waltzes	C.E. Vandersloot	Vandersloot Music Co., New York
	Little Zulu Lu	Dave Reed Jr.	M. Witmark and Sons, New York
	My Wheel Napoleon	H.S. Bott and J.C. Beckel	Bonanza Music Pub., Philadelphia
	New York and	E.T. Paull	E.T. Paull Music, New York
	Coney Island Cycle March		
	The Referee March	Ben C. Brown	C.C. Brown, Vivoqua, Wisconsin
	The Scorcher	Hayes and Hayes	M.F. Hayes, New York
	Sweetheart, I Love None But You	H. Perlet	N. Weinstein, New York
	The Southern Wheelmen's March	Voges and Stoddard	Werlein, New Orleans
	Up a Tree March	J.I. Alexander	Perry Brothers, Philadelphia
	Wheeling Together	A. Craig and Quinn	El Dorando Cycle Co., Chicago
	Wheeling - Waltz Song	H. Wakefield Smith	H.W. Smith, Buffalo
1897	Bang, Bang, Bang	Connor	F.A. Mills, California
	Went the Rubber Tire		
	Bicycle Bell	John C. Gabler	Wm. A. Pond, New York
	Bicycle Race - Galop	Eduard Holst	McKinley Music Co., New York
	The Chaser - Two Step	Frank Banta	W.B. Gray and Co., New York
	The Crackerjack March	John C. Schuler	John C. Schuler, Buffalo
	The Cyclists National Grand March	George Maywood	Imperial Music Co., New York
	and Two Step		

164

Year	Title	Composer	Publisher
	Dora Brown	Nellie Burt	Geo. L. Spaulding, New York
	Lafayette Two Step	M. Barnard	Will Rossiter, New York
	The L.A.W. Scorcher	George Rosey	Jos W. Stern and Co., New York
	Ma Caline	Ben Tuttle	Lyn and Healy, Chicago
	The Merry Cycle Girl	Cleaver and Reifsnyder	Zabel-Worley, Philadelphia
	The Neverout March	F. Ibsen	Rose Manufacturing Co., Philadelphia
	Pretty Polly Palmer	Arthur Sheldon	M. Witmark and Sons, New York
	Queen of the Bicycle Girls	Gardner and Langey	Press of Philadelphia
	When the Boys and Girls Go Wheeling	Browne and Coleman	Coleman, New York
	The Stout Man's Conquest	Walter Phillips	G. Monroe Sons, New York
	The Roof Garden Cycle Party	S.B. Alexander	M. Witmark, New York
	On the Boulevard	Joseph E. Howard	Chas. K. Harris, New York
	My Little May	Chas K. Champ	Broder and Schlam, New York
1898	The A.W.C. March and Two Step	Harry E. Jeroy	Harry E. Jeroy, Bridgeport
	Cyclist's March	E.B. Kursheedt	I. Prager, New York
	Kelly's Bicycle Song	John T. Kelly	T.B. Harms and Co., New York
	Lily Crow	P.W. Eaton and M.B. Upperman	Hitchcock Pub., New York
	Mary Ellen Simpkins Bike	Abbott and Norman	T.B. Harms and Co., New York
	The Pretty Little Scorcher	George Rosey and Dave Reed	Joseph W. Stern, New York
	She's Got My Eyes	Augusta Howe Chambers	C. Coleman, Brooklyn
	The Talk of the Town	Harry Zickel	Zickel Bros., Detroit
	White Heather Two Step	Manuel Klein	Howley Haviland Co., New York
1899	Alabama Hot Stuff	George Goldthwaite	Sherman Music Co., Boston
	An Easy Mark	Samuel H. Speck	Enterprise Music, New York
	A Florida Cracker - Rag Two Step	Ellis Brooks	S. Brainards Sons New York
	The Wench That Rides a Wheel	Moody and Grabbe	Grabbe Music Pub., Davenport
	Wheelmans Song	E.S. Neil	G.C. Shepard Co., Winchester, Virginia
	American Wheelmen's March	T.W. Erwin	J.F. Bellois, Philadelphia
1900	Pretty Jessie Moore	Geo. L. Spaulding	New York Journal
1901	Cycling Song	Rolleston and Barrett	University Song Book
1902	Daredevil	Laurent J. Tonnele	Peerless Publishing, New York
	America Up to Date	J.S. Duss	New York, American Supplement
1904	Mr. Dike From Pike	Eugene Ellsworth	M. Witmark And Sons, New York
1934	Back in Those Bicycle Days	Allan and Manoloff	M.M. Cole Pub. Chicago
1936	Pedal Your Blues Away	Wells, Griffin and Miller	Bob Miller, New York
1937	Sing a Song of Safety	Gerald Marks	Irving Caesar, New York
1940	My Bicycle Girl	Hammerstein and Schwartz	Chappell Music Co., New York